THE
FUTURE
AS
HISTORY

*the text of this book is printed
on 100% recycled paper*

THE
FUTURE
AS
HISTORY

The historic currents of our time and the
direction in which they are taking America

BY

ROBERT L. HEILBRONER

HARPER TORCHBOOKS
Harper & Row, Publishers
New York, Hagerstown, San Francisco, London

For Peter and David

CONTENTS

I

—»» ««—

THE
ENCOUNTER
WITH
HISTORY

1. *The Shock of Events*

History, as it comes into our daily lives, is charged with surprise and shock. When we think back over the past few years, what strikes us is the suddenness of its blows, the unannounced descent of its thunderbolts. Wars, revolutions, uprisings have burst upon us with terrible rapidity. Advances in science and technology have rewritten the very terms and conditions of the human contract with no more warning than the morning's headlines. Encompassing social and economic changes have not only unalterably rearranged our lives, but seem to have done so behind our backs, while we were not looking.

These recurring surprises and shocks of contemporary history throw a pall of chronic apprehensiveness over our times. Reading the morning newspaper has become an act no longer anticipated with mild pleasure but with uneasy suspense. The bewildering turnabouts of fortune, the abrupt shifts of expectations, the awareness of the innumerable microscopic factors by which our destiny may be affected, all conspire to make of our encounter with history a frightening and disorienting ordeal.

In themselves the genuine threats and dangers of individual

events provide sufficient reason for this pervasive anxiety. But in the aggregate, the sweep of events presents us with a still more profoundly upsetting experience. To review the course of world history over the past quarter century is to call to mind a period of historic assault such as we have never known before. No more than thirty years ago, the United States represented a form of economic and political society whose prospects and permanence were unquestioned. Today we find ourselves in a position of defensive insecurity. Who would have denied the brilliance of the outlook for the United States during the first quarter of the twentieth century? Who can confidently assert as much in the century's middle years?

This assault of history has not been confined to our international position. At home we have also watched the train of affairs take an unexpected and generally unwelcome turning. Within our own nation we have seen the emergence of a society—massively organized and bureaucratic in its private as well as in its public institutions—which is neither entirely to our liking, nor what is worse, entirely of our conscious making.

All these adverse experiences of recent decades, some sharp and dramatic, others subtle and surreptitious, add to our contemporary feeling of unease and confusion. We feel ourselves beleaguered by happenings which seem not only malign and intransigent, but unpredictable. We are at a loss to know how to anticipate the events the future may bring or how to account for those events once they have happened. The future itself is a direction in which we look no longer with confidence but with vague forebodings and a sense of unpreparedness.

Yet this generalized anxiety before the future describes

rather than accounts for our contemporary mood. The core of our inquietude stems from a more fundamental condition than the feeling of unpreparedness which is only its most acutely felt symptom. At bottom our troubled state of mind reflects an inability to see the future in an *historic* context. If current events strike us as all surprise and shock it is because we cannot see these events in a meaningful framework. If the future seems to us a kind of limbo, a repository of endless surprises, it is because we no longer see it as the expected culmination of the past, as the growing edge of the present. More than anything else, our disorientation before the future reveals a loss of our historic identity, an incapacity to grasp our historic situation. Unlike our forefathers who lived very much *in* history and *for* history, we ourselves appear to be adrift in an historic void.

Yet we are all aware that we do not live in such a void. Looking backward we can see that the past seemed as full of contingency to its contemporaries as the present and future do to us, but despite this we are used to finding orderliness in the history which our forbears "made" out of the spectrum of possibilities before them. Looking forward we can also recognize, however imprecisely, the presence of "forces" at work in the world, whose impact on our destiny is neither wholly arbitrary nor wholly unpredictable.

The problem, then, is to establish a sense of order and continuity in the face of the historic realities which confront us. It is to re-establish our encounter with history as part of the living momentum of our age rather than as a blind plunge into the unknown. Needless to say, this does not mean that history is foreseeable in its infinite detail. Much of the intimate minutiae of history—those minutiae which spell the joy and sorrow of our individual lives—must remain unknowable. But the fact that the future is inscrutable for each of us individually does not mean that it is equally impenetrable for all of us collectively. As individuals we move into the future on the mingled accident and design of our lives. As a society we move into the future on the grand dynamic of history. It is this grandiose design which we must discover if we are to comprehend the meaning of the struggles of our time.

2. *Optimism and the Idea of the Future*

What this dynamic of contemporary history may be is a matter with which this whole book is concerned. But at the outset an important problem must be faced. It is the fact that the very notion of an "historic" future is one which most Americans are apt to find uncomfortable. Our national temperament inclines us in quite another direction. We are naturally sympathetic to ideas which stress the plasticity and promise, the openness of the future, and impatient with views which emphasize the "fated" aspect of human affairs. We strive to see in the challenges which beset us not obstacles but opportunities. In a word, we are an optimistic people.

When it is called to our attention in this fashion, we tend

to conceive of our traditional optimism as a *personal* philosophy—as a character trait which sets our aspirations above the horizons of private circumstance. Thus we often overlook something which is much more fundamental. This is the fact that an attitude of optimism, for all its emphasis on personal striving and accomplishment, does not ultimately rest on a judgment about our private capabilities. It rests on a judgment about our historic capacities. At bottom, *a philosophy of optimism is an historic attitude toward the future*—an attitude based on the tacit premise that the future will accommodate the striving which we bring to it. Optimism is grounded in the faith that the historic environment, as it comes into being, will prove to be benign and congenial—or at least neutral to our private efforts.

This is so unpresuming an assumption that it comes as something of a shock to recognize that over most of human history it has been untenable. Optimism as a philosophy of life, as an attitude toward history, is a phenomenon which we find restricted to a minute period of historic time and geographic space. Indeed as an enduring trait of national character it could almost be called exclusively American. This is not because other men have been less desirous than Americans of looking upon the affirmative side of life's problems. Rather, as we shall see, it is because the expression and sanction of those hopes in a philosophy of confident expectations would not have been compatible with their experience.

Thus both the presence of our own optimistic bent, and the absence of one elsewhere, is testimony to the historic situations in which those traits of character were formed. Just as in our own case optimism reflects an experience with history in

which any less confident and bold philosophy would have
failed to measure up to reality, so in the case of the rest of
the world the absence of a native optimism mirrors an experience with history very different from ours. The future
over most of mankind's experience has not been that benign
and congenial environment which we unthinkingly anticipate
it to be, but has been formidable and overwhelming, unalter-
able and often unanswerable.

3.   *The Future as the Mirror of the Past*

It is difficult for us to imagine the state of mind that such
an exposure to history might have given rise to. But no sooner
do we attempt to capture this state of mind than an unexpected
fact attracts our notice. It is that over by far the greater part
of man's existence the importance of the future assumed much
smaller proportions than it does in our day. Indeed, until a few
centuries ago in the West, and until relatively recent times in
the East, it was the past and not the future which was the
dominant orientation to historic time. Modern man, who
typically sets his life goals in what is to come, displays an attitude quite the converse of earlier days. Ancient Egypt,
Greece, Rome, the vast Asiatic civilizations, even the Renais-
sance, did not look ahead for the ideals and inspirations of

their existence, but sought them in their origins, in their ancient glories, their fabled heroes, their pristine virtues real or fancied. Unlike modern man, who dreams of the world he will make, pre-modern man dreamed of the world he left.

It was not by preference that mankind dwelt upon its past. The orientation was itself a reflection of a basic condition of existence. That condition was mankind's stasis, its change-lessness, its inertness. To be sure, the immediate pageant of what we usually call "history" was marked with all its triumphs and tragedies, its turns and twists; while from our now remote vantage point we can discern the rise and fall of larger tides of cultures and civilizations. But from the point of view of the anonymous millions who constituted those societies, neither the pageants nor the tides were such that daily life could be reliably harnessed to them. At the apex of society the powerful few, like the very gods, carried on their sport, now beneficently, now calamitously, but always inscrutably; at the base of society, if there were glacial drifts, they were no more noticeable than that. It is but a slight error, if error it be at all, to picture the life horizons of the overwhelming majority of men in fifteenth-century Europe as essentially unchanged from what they had been in fifth-century B.C. Greece, or the experience of existence for the Asian cultivator of 1900 as in no significant way elevated over that of his remote forbears two thousand years before. Certainly whatever elevation there had been was to be measured, not by generations, but by centuries.

Against such an eternally unchanging backdrop of life, it is not surprising that the idea of the future played a far smaller role than we invest it with. In the viselike clamp of reality, hopeful anticipations of the future were never given room to expand. The granitic facts of nature, the simple biological continuity of the human community, were accepted as they were, and the idea that the facts might be altered, that the simple continuity might give way to a dynamic and foreseeable improvement, did not enter within the ambit of beliefs.

Hence, to the extent that the future was of meaningful interest, it was only as the ever-changing, but never-changed battle in which man contested with his fate. Like a Greek frieze, such a future was organized around the heroic exploits of great men, but these exploits, while their outcome was ever in doubt, did not constitute an essential departure from the past. Kings succeeded kings, empires followed on empires, but so far as the perception of contemporaries was concerned "history" was a succession of changes whose main attribute was their violence, not their aggregate evolution. "The only thing," writes the historian Collingwood, "that a shrewd and critical Greek like Herodotus would say about the divine power that ordains the course of history is that . . . it rejoices in upsetting and disturbing things."[1]

To come to grips with such a capricious but withal monotonous future, the ancients turned to the factor which was common in all its permutations. This was the factor of human motivation and especially of heroic motivation. Thus it was envy and loyalty, love and hate, power and submissiveness—in short the primordium of human nature—which were thought to contain the impelling force of events. And thus too, when pre-modern man sought to divine the course of things to come, he sought for it in the rationale of things past. As Machiavelli

[1] R. G. Collingwood, *The Idea of History* (New York, 1956). p. 22.

wrote, ". . . whoever wishes to foresee the future must consult the past; for human events ever resemble those of preceding times. This arises from the fact that they are produced by men who ever have been, and ever will be, animated by the same passions, and thus they necessarily have the same results."[2]

What was so egregiously lacking in this estimate of the future was a central conception of modern life: the idea of social movement, of aggregate betterment, of progress. It is astonishing when we look back upon the infinitely painful panorama of past history to find that this idea is totally absent as a popular sentiment. Pre-modern man could console himself for the harsh realities of existence in his visions of heaven, he could gratefully accept the social reforms handed down from time to time by his compassionate masters, he could indulge in sporadic and short-lived outbreaks of despair. What he could not bring himself to believe was that heaven might be sought on earth, that reform might proceed from his own aspirations, that despair could give way to determination.

And yet the very splendor of his religious images tells us that his inability to conceive for himself a bright future was not due to a lack of imagination, just as his fortitude in life tells us that it was not due to a failure of will. What lacked were requisites of a much more mundane kind. First there was needed the power to alter man's subservience before nature to a mastery of it. Second, there was required a belief in the legitimacy of the idea of human betterment. And last there was missing a framework of social institutions which would combine power and hope, and which would then permit this fruitful combination to achieve its own spontaneous growth.

[2] *Discourses*, Book Three, Chap. XLIII; see also Book One, Chap. XXXIX.

4. *The Forces of Change Emerge*

As a confluence of three great rivers of human development, the requisites came with a rush, beginning with the seventeenth century, and together they literally swept man from his historic moorings. Within a century the past had changed from a source of inspiration to a collection of mistakes, and the future, hitherto so featureless, had risen up like a Promised Land. By the eighteenth century, an immense optimism had swept over Europe, and no one voiced it so enthusiastically as the philosopher-historian Condorcet: "There is no limit set to the perfecting of the powers of man," he wrote. "The progress of this perfectibility, henceforth independent of any power that might wish to stop it, has no other limit than the duration of the globe upon which nature had placed us. Doubtless this progress can proceed at a pace more or less rapid, but it will never go backward; at least," the philosopher adds circumspectly, "so long as the earth occupies the same place in the system of the universe. . . ."[3]

Within the limits of this essay it is impossible to do full justice to the revolutionary developments in which such senti-

[3] Condorcet, *Progrès de l'esprit humain*, Intro. to Epoque I.

22

ments were grounded. But at least we must understand that the Enlightenment, with its sublime confidence in reason and progress, was not merely a movement that materialized out of thin air.

It coincided, in the first place, with an immediate and tangible harbinger of change—that gathering cluster of inventive and scientific thought whose culmination we call the Industrial Revolution. Throughout the seventeenth century a steadily accelerating tempo of discovery—and more important than that, of systematic *search*—began to set into motion a chain of technological achievements whose effect in altering the visible face of society would be greater over the next two hundred years than all the technical progress of the preceding two thousand.

Needless to say, the preparations for this flowering had been long in the making. But what had previously marked their extended history had been the lack of any concerted drive to apply science and technology to the conditions of ordinary life. Greek science was a dazzling accomplishment of the mind, but it alleviated only very little the duress of the body, whose more onerous tasks were borne mainly by slaves. The most amazing achievements in the architecture of Rome were accompanied by an almost total disinterest in the technology of her basic material mode of existence—agriculture—with the result that the introduction of such simple and fundamental improvements as the wheeled plow or an efficient horse-collar would wait until the Middle Ages. Even Leonardo's extraordinary genius anticipated rather than ushered in a basic improvement in the technology of workaday life, and either the notebooks which later generations would find crammed with the most fruitful ideas were unknown to his own generation, or their broad-scale suggestions were passed over in favor of his mechanical fancies or his imaginative inventions of war.

In contrast, what gave to the nascent Industrial Revolution its truly revolutionary character was not alone the fecundity of ideas and the newness of the machines it produced, but their large-scale economic applicability. Inventions such as the power loom and the steam engine could no longer be said merely to decorate the surface of life. They penetrated to a hitherto ignored substratum of existence—its foundation of common labor. For the first time in history, the productivity of common toil was itself made the focus of systematic investigation. The consequences, in terms of man's conception of his environment, were of incalculable magnitude. Nature, which had hitherto been the master of man, now became his great slave.

Second only to this epoch-making industrial transformation, a political change infused the future with a new hopefulness. This was the movement which began with the English and culminated in the French and American revolutions.

As with the Industrial Revolution, the great political breakthroughs of the eighteenth century could trace a distant ancestry: ancient Greece had known its famous but strictly limited political democracy, and Rome had had its short-lived proletarian upheavals. But until the political ferment of the Age of Reason, the notion of democratic equality was largely confined to a feeling of religious brotherhood. And the fact that Christians had professed to feel themselves alike in the sight of God by no means implied the idea that they were alike in the sight of each other. Until the great uprisings of the seventeenth and eighteenth centuries the commonalty of man was never admitted to an equal footing with its lords and masters. "It is seemly," wrote Ramón Lull in the late thirteenth-century *Book of the Order of Chivalry*, "that the men should plough and dig and work hard, in order that the earth may yield the fruits from which the knight and his horse will live; and that the knight, who rides and does a lord's work, should get his wealth from the things on which his men are to spend much toil and fatigue."[4]

It was only very gradually that even burgher, petty capitalist, and merchant saw in the exercise of political power a prerogative which might be legitimately theirs; and even they, in the revolutions which legitimized their aspirations, did not realize that what they had done, in confirming their own right to power, was to open the way of legitimacy for the political aspirations of "the men" beneath them. Thus, as the technical achievements of the age dismantled the material barriers of the future, the political achievements dismantled its barriers of privilege. The future now harbored the intoxicating notion that henceforth *everyone* might seek to advance, the poor along with the rich, the weak with the strong.

But these new and sanguine expectations for the future yet required a social and economic mechanism by which they could be put into effect; and this final requisite found its realization in the gradual development of capitalism itself.

What emergent capitalism added to the power of the new technology and to the impetus of the new aspirations was a social framework in which the expansive tendencies of each were brought into complementary harness. For the first time

[4] *Cambridge Economic History*, vol. I, p. 277.

the energies of a hitherto marginal group, the brash, adventure-some, upstart manufacturing enterprisers, found both the technical means and the political and social climate for full-scale development. The artisan James Watt and the self-educated potter's son, Josiah Wedgwood; the clockmaker Benjamin Huntsman who turned to steelmaking; and the barber Richard Arkwright who filched the secret of the spinning jenny and thereupon built himself an immense textile empire—these were the humble men who found in capitalism an avenue for talents that in a different organization of society would have been smothered.

It was not, of course, only the new men who gave capitalism its immense forward push. It was the system under which the Watts and Wedgwoods, Huntsmans and Arkwrights were set one against the other in a contest on which society imposed no restraints except those of the impersonal market place. As a result capitalism literally galvanized the pace of technological and economic progress. In *The Communist Manifesto*, Marx and Engels have written perhaps the most famous eulogy of its achievements:

> The bourgeoisie, during its rule of scarce one hundred years, has created more massive and more colossal productive forces than have all preceding generations together. Subjugation of nature's forces to man, machinery, application of chemistry to industry and agriculture, steam-navigation, railways, electric telegraphs, clearing of whole continents for cultivation, canalization of rivers, whole populations conjured out of the ground—what earlier century had even a presentiment that such productive forces slumbered in the lap of social labour?

What interests us here is not the detailed history of these new currents of social change. It is the fact that the emergence of the forces of technology, politics, and economics was responsible for a polar change of attitude toward human existence. For the first time men began to speculate about the future in terms of a rising level of *mass* well-being, intelligence, and ideals. Ideas of scientific and social advance, of that perfectibility of man which, as Condorcet had put it, would take place "independent of any power that might wish to stop it"— all this infused the air with an attitude of buoyant expectations. One cannot say that a single cohesive "philosophy of optimism" was born. But there was a confidence in the ultimate beneficence of what was to come, unlike any attitude to the secular future man had ever known before. Saint-Just, Robespierre's young colleague, summed up the age in a poignant phrase: Happiness, he said, was a new idea in Europe.

5. *The New Conception of History*

It was not only happiness which was a new idea. With the change in the reality of mankind's situation, there came as well a new conception of "history" itself. Previously, as we have seen, the word mainly connoted to its contemporaries the course of the dynastic and military, the political and personal fate of the heroes of society. What lay beneath this pageant was deemed essentially uninteresting, "unhistoric"— except insofar as the masses responded to stimuli from above. But now the meaning of history changed in the consciousness of those who were experiencing it. In a very real sense, "society" discovered itself. The content of history—which is to say, the matters that concerned those who were thoughtful about history—expanded to include aspects of human life which had never heretofore merited the historian's glance. "The thing I want to see," wrote Carlyle in the first flush of this new perspective, "is not Red-Book lists of Court Calendars and Parliamentary Registers, but the Life of Man in England."

With this shift in the "substance" of history came as well a change in the identification of the mechanisms that "made" the new social history. As the center of historical interest moved from the foreground of the stage to the background, as the Life of Man took precedence over that of history's heroes, the traditional motives and agents of history were supplanted by new ones. For the exploits of great individuals, hitherto so decisive for the events of a heroic history, were inadequate to account for a new conception of history whose campaigns were fought with technology, mass political movement, and the laws of capitalist evolution. In a word, the idea of social history brought to the fore a new determinant of historic development: no longer heroic will, but *historic force*.

The awareness of history-making "forces" as such was not new, of course. Whether before the wrath of the gods, or the dictates of climate and geography, men had always admitted limits to the control which even heroic action exercised over their destinies. The pressure of environment was always accorded a large, if silent, role in the conception of any people's history, and the exaltation of the hero had always been counterbalanced by that of fate.

What *was* newly contained in the historic philosophy of optimism was the idea that this exterior pressure of history might be rooted not in the strictures of nature or the whims of the gods, but in the mass actions of men themselves. For the introduction of technology, democratic aspiration, and economic activity into the center of history-*making* brought with them a fragmentation of history's motive forces: no longer was it the large-scale individual acts of rulers that provided the "force" of these new currents of social change, but rather the small-scale actions of thousands or even millions of human beings, integrating themselves into an anonymous agency of social change. To be sure, there were heroes of technology, popular political action, and capitalism just as there had been heroes of war or dynastic contest. But important as a Newton, a Robespierre, or an Arkwright might be, the impetus of the forces they represented and advanced did not reside primarily in them, as the success or failure of a dynasty or a campaign might reside in a prince or a great general. At bottom it was the spread of political ideas from mind to mind, of economic pressure from market to market, of scientific advance from laboratory to laboratory which provided the metabolism of social growth and change.

It was not that *all* of history was thought to be determined by these newly identified social forces. Those facets of experience which had previously most interested their contemporaries—the accidents of war, the careers of rulers, what Karl Popper calls "that history of international crime and mass

murder which has been advertised as the history of mankind"
—all these strands of history remained as "open," as "heroic,"
as "personal" as before. What was critical, however, was that
the web woven of these traditional strands was now regarded
as less pertinent to the "Life of Man," less charged with fundamental consequences for the future, than that formed by the
new agents of historic change.

6. *The Inevitability of Progress*

But another and more important consequence followed as
the main thrust of history became lodged in its anonymous
social forces. Because these forces were the expression of mass
human activity and of widely diffused ideas and beliefs, their
appearance and operation within society took on a wholly new
guise from that of heroic history-making. Real enough to
mean bankruptcy or the guillotine, as tangible as industrial
machinery or as visible as the newly affluent manufacturing
class, the forces of social history nonetheless presented a
strangely elusive reality. They seemed to defy—or at any rate
to stand above—the power of individuals to influence their
course. There was no simple riddance to the power of a
dangerous political idea; no assassination possible to avert a
disruptive change in technology; no natural death to be

counted on to stop an economic change that ripped up ancestral estates or stirred up class discontent. The carriers of these forces were too many to be dealt with individually; the history they carried seemed to display a momentum of its own.

Hence the new agents of history's advance brought with them an undertone of inexorability, of relentlessness, of social causation and social process as determinate as physical causation or physical process.

And with this new "determinism" of social history came yet one final and most important change of all. It was a new method of looking into the future. Heretofore, when men had looked ahead, they had had to rely on prophecy or insight or on sheer flights of intellectual speculation. But now, with the rising importance accorded to the forces of history, a new manner of foreseeing the future suggested itself to the age. The future appeared to be *predictable*.

For an age brought up on Newtonian mechanics was not long in seeing the resemblance between a physical universe of interacting particles and a social universe of interacting human beings. The very dissolution of history's momentum into individually insignificant atoms of political belief, into invisible currents of a scientific "turn of mind," into an economic pulverization of action over a thousand markets—all this strongly suggested an analogy to the predictable behavior of physical entities. In the celestial universe, for example, a similar multitude of particles and motions had revealed themselves to the astronomers as bound by order and discipline: was it not reasonable, then, that within the universe of men a similar lawfulness would reveal itself to the social astronomer? As the

Abbé Mably, an eighteenth-century *philosophe*, put it: "Is Society, then, a branch of Physics?"

It was pre-eminently the new "science" of economics to which fell the task of discovering and describing the motions of the social universe. For economics—or Political Arithmetick, as it was revealingly called in its formative stages—did indeed treat of the internal motions of society in a manner which made the future a matter of determinable calculation. In the eyes of the economist, society was composed of innumerable particles of humanity, each one of whom was strongly polarized toward profit and away from loss, and all of whom were thrown together on the market place to fare as best they could. The outcome of such a struggle was clearly not an arbitrary arrangement of the particles. As mysteriously, and yet as ineluctably as the forces of magnetism aligned iron filings, so the forces of competition, of ever-opening opportunities for money-making, of the pressure of population upon the labor market all operated to guide the human particles to predictable patterns of behavior. As a result economics could deduce the adjustments which the human particles were continually *forced* to make, and could foresee in advance the relationships that would inevitably take place between class and class and the changes that would affect the community as a whole.

No single work so fully epitomized this new foresight as Adam Smith's *Wealth of Nations*, published in the year of the American Revolution. In Adam Smith's great conception, an "invisible hand" directed the mass of individuals to their posts —and, beyond this, directed the entirety of society toward its economic destiny. The economic mechanism as a whole was thus embarked on a long upward gradient whose prospects stretched far into the future, and whose slow but perceptible benefits attended even the meanest of society's classes. And all of this propitious vista needed for its realization nothing more than a continuation of the economic process to which men were in any case driven and from which they could not escape.

Hence Smith was a believer in progress, but progress of a very different sort from that envisioned by Condorcet. It was not the perfectibility of man but only the acquisitiveness of shopkeepers which propelled Smith's social vehicle in the direction of wealth and improvement. It was not the benevolence of the butcher or the baker on which he banked his hopes, but only the likelihood that they would continue to follow their narrow self-interest. In the *Wealth of Nations* progress was no longer an idealistic goal of mankind, but only a destination to which it was driven willy-nilly; it was not a conscious purpose of social activity, but only a by-product of private economic aims.

Yet if Smith's optimism thereby lost much of the nobility of that of Condorcet, what it gained was the inestimable strength of certitude. It was not a passionate though vague sense of great possibilities which lifted Smith's hopes, but the cold alchemy of the forces of history, working indifferently and impersonally to create an environment of human betterment. Progress was thus no longer a matter of hopefulness. It was a matter of predictable evolution. Under the determinism of the economic process, progress had become inevitable.

The idea of the inevitability of progress sheds an important light on the philosophy of optimism whose roots we have been endeavoring to unearth. It makes evident the fact that a hopeful orientation toward the future did not emerge solely from confidence in man's unaided ability to shape his own destiny. On the contrary, it came with the growth of historic forces which promised to shape his destiny for him. It was the dynamic potential of technology and of democratic aspiration, brought to fruition within a self-sustaining mechanism for economic growth, which first opened the future to optimistic expectation; and further yet it was the very blindness, the determinism of these forces which fortified men's faith in them.

But an understanding of this deterministic core of the optimistic philosophy has more than an historic interest and relevance. It bears directly on our contemporary philosophy of expectations. For it enables us to see that optimism, despite its celebration of personal striving, does not reject the idea of the future "as history." Rather, it stems directly from an historic view of the future. Indeed, it is difficult to conceive of an optimistic philosophy which does not draw its faith from the ongoing momentum of historic forces. What optimism does assume about the future is not an *absence* of historic influence, but a *congeniality* of influence. Or to put it differently, a philosophy of optimism assumes that the direction in which we seek to venture as the heroic steersmen of our destiny will be compatible with the currents and tides set in motion by history's impersonal forces.

This understanding has yet a further consequence. It makes clear that the philosophy of optimism, in binding us to a tacit acceptance of history's forces, also binds us to certain conceptions *about* history's forces. What these conceptions may be, and the manner in which they condition our outlook, thus become matters which it is essential for us to ascertain. And for this there is no better way than to follow the fortunes of the optimistic philosophy, first to its unhappy demise in Europe and then to its uneasy trial in the United States today.

7. *The Waning of Confidence*

In Europe the philosophy of optimism lasted for over a century. In part it was no more than the natural expression of the contentment of an age in which the fortunes of the classes above the working level improved rapidly: between 1815 and 1830, for instance, it has been estimated that the purchasing power of the English middle and upper-middle classes virtually doubled. But at least as important as the actual improvement was the continuing belief that this improvement followed from a current of progress to which society was now firmly hitched. "Human history is a record of progress—a record of accumulating knowledge and increasing wisdom, of continual advancement from a lower to a higher platform of intelligence and well-being," wrote a minor but much reprinted historian of the 1880's; "The growth of man's well-being, rescued from the mischievous tampering of self-willed princes, is left now to the beneficent regulation of great providential laws."[5]

[5] From Collingwood, *op. cit.*, p. 146.

And yet the philosophy of optimism was curiously defensive almost from the outset. An undercurrent of dissent—and worse, of disillusion—soon began to cut away beneath the prevailing air of confidence. For, at least in the eyes of some of its more critical contemporary observers, a tragic betrayal of hopes was taking place. It was not that the new forces of industrialism, of democracy, of capitalism failed to assert their predicted historic influence. It was rather that the consequences of that influence were quite different from those which an earlier generation had pictured.

To begin with, the new industrial technology had scarce begun to show its promise before another and uglier aspect of itself was revealed. Arkwright's spinning jenny, for example, became not merely an implement to increase many-fold the output of cotton wares, but also a monster to be tended by undernourished children. The son of the Duc de la Rochefoucauld-Liancourt, visiting the Paisley mills in 1793 reported on their lot: "They work twelve hours straight off, without the necessary intervals for food and rest. When they have finished they are immediately relieved so that work only ceases on Sundays. . . . I inquired whether this work did not have ill effects on their health, but I was assured that this was not so."[6]

It was not alone the abuses of the factory system which dismayed the more critical minds of the day. It was the system itself: the trooping to work of industrial pygmies in a landscape of hell; the trooping home from work to the disease and filth-ridden slums of the industrial cities; and not least

[6] From P. Mantoux, *The Industrial Revolution in the 18th Century* (London, 1928), p. 424n.

the draining from work of everything in it which was human, until man was used only as a machine. Adam Smith himself had warned: "The man whose whole life is spent in performing a few simple operations . . . has no occasion to exert his understanding. . . . He naturally loses, therefore, the habit of such exertion, and generally becomes as stupid and ignorant as it is possible for a human being to become."[7]

Hence from the beginning, within the force of technological progress was divined a component whose untoward social repercussions might vitiate the sheerly physical gains of the new productivity. Marx was later to expound this as the "alienation" which attends labor in an industrial system. But long before the industrial system reached its full scale of impersonal organization it had exercised many minds to doubt the "beneficent regulation of great providential laws." As Thomas Arnold, the headmaster of Rugby, wrote before the mid-century: "A man sets up a factory and *wants hands;* I beseech you, sir, to observe the very expressions that are used, for they are all significant. What he wants of his fellow creatures is the loan of their hands; of their heads and hearts he thinks nothing."[8]

Meanwhile another current of disillusion began to manifest itself toward the historic forces of progress represented by the trend toward political equality. For the enfranchisement of the people did not bring with it an unequivocal improvement over the "meddlesome tampering" of princes. Indeed, to unsympathetic observers, such as Burke, or later Carlyle, the legitimization of the popular will promised little more than

[7] *Wealth of Nations* (Modern Library ed.), p. 734.
[8] J. L. and Barbara Hammond, *The Bleak Age* (London, 1934), p. 45.

the licensing of the Terror of the French Revolution—a terror which, ironically enough, drove Condorcet to suicide in order to escape the guillotine.

But it was not just a rapid disenchantment with the ability of the people to govern themselves which chastened optimistic sentiment; it was also an increasingly perturbed evaluation of another aspect of democracy—that of the mass mind. Even such political liberals as John Stuart Mill or De Tocqueville expressed their fears and reservations before the prospect of intellectual and cultural egalitarianism. "The public has . . . among a democratic people a singular power, of which aristocratic nations could never so much as conceive an idea"; wrote the latter, "for it does not persuade to certain opinions, but it enforces them, and infuses them into the faculties by a sort of enormous pressure of the minds of all upon the reason of each."[9] More brutally and with an overt ill will, Nietzsche said the same thing: "I am opposed to parliamentary government and to the power of the press," he wrote in *The Will to Power*, "because they are the means whereby cattle become masters."

And yet the crux of the gathering disillusion with the philosophy of optimism was not founded on these disappointments so much as on a third: the performance of the capitalist system as the vehicle of the historic future.

For it was capitalism which pre-eminently represented the *automatic* achievement of progress. And whereas it was soon clear that capitalism had unquestionably changed economic conditions, it was far from evident that it had improved them —at least for the new hero of history, the common man. "The

---

[9] *Democracy in America* (World's Classics ed., 1947), p. 298.

following description is an impartial and accurate one of the present situation of the population of Great Britain which lives by working in the manufacturing industries," wrote a liberal economist of the 1840's. "When trade is normal about a third of the population lives in terrible poverty and on the verge of starvation. A second third, perhaps even more, earns little more than the ordinary rural worker. Only one-third receives wages which allow them a fairly reasonable standard of life and a little comfort."[10] It was an indictment to be many times documented; it would not be until 1875, according to the calculations of Arnold Toynbee, Sr.—not until a century after the publication of the *Wealth of Nations*—that the common laborer in England in the course of his ordinary employment would earn enough to provide a decent subsistence.

Even more distressing than the lamentable pace of advance was the growing belief that the *direction* of movement no longer seemed to point assuredly toward an optimistic goal. For the determinism of economic "law," in the hands of economists other than Adam Smith, now gave reason to suspect that the automatic mechanism of society might prove to be not a machine for social advance, but merely one for social grinding, or possibly even for retrograde motion. Scarcely a generation after Smith's explication of the great ascent, Malthus had dealt a stunning blow to social expectations by propounding his dilemma of the tendency of population to outrun the means of subsistence. Shortly thereafter, David Ricardo elaborated that theme into a rigorous economic analysis which envisaged as the fate of society nothing more hopeful than the steady enrichment of the landlord at the expense of

[10] From F. Sternberg, *Capitalism and Socialism on Trial*, p. 55.

worker and capitalist alike. Thus the determinism which had served the cause of optimism so well under a benign interpretation of its laws by Adam Smith now presented society with an inexorable outlook of a very different sort.

Needless to say, the tide of pessimistic readings of the historic future further unsettled the prevailing optimism. It inspired movements of social protest which fluttered the Victorian pulse with the specter of socialism in a dozen different guises. For the first time the prevailing order felt itself threatened, and an anxious sensitivity to radicalism appeared.

In point of fact, the socialist reformers were hopelessly weak and divided and the political threat they posed to the established order was marginal. But philosophically their differences merged to offer a concerted challenge to the beliefs of the age. For all the reformers agreed that capitalism, *left to itself*, would not be the vehicle of a "naturally improving" future. All agreed that if true social progress were to be achieved history would have to be reshaped for the better *against* the onrush of its own uncontrolled forces.

8. *The Marxian Blow*

Curiously, it is this widening abandonment of faith in *deterministic* progress which, in retrospect, makes Karl Marx so important in the intellectual history of optimistic thought. For unlike his radical contemporaries Marx did not call for an opposition to the forces of history. On the contrary he accepted all of them, the drive of technology, the revolutionizing effects of democratic striving, even the vagaries of capitalism, as being indeed the carriers of a brighter future. The difference was that he envisaged this future as lying beyond the confines of the existing structure of society. To Marx, one last barrier had to be crossed before the promise of history would be fulfilled. That was the overthrow of the outmoded system of private production, and the passage through a transition of socialism into the ultimate communist destination of social history. The achievement of the communist revolution—itself both a "heroic" act and an "inevitable" culmination of the forces inherent in history—was thus to be the true realization of the optimistic content of the present.

We must notice about the Marxian view that it was not the element of economic determinism in its analysis which was inimical to the bourgeois outlook. Rather it was the bold application of determinism *beyond* the confines of the economic process proper. The classical economists had been every bit as deterministic as Marx, and some of them had reached conclusions as dark as his. But they had never thought to connect the foreseeable evolution of the economy with its larger *social* matrix. Hence their predictions, however gloomy, had a certain saving reassurance in that they never involved the stability of the social order. Ricardo, for example, writing with near-mathematical logic on the impending squeeze on worker and capitalist in favor of the fattening landlord, never suggested that such a process might set up intolerable social pressures which would end by exploding the landlord.

In contradistinction, Marx's major contribution to historic thought was his insistence that the economy was inextricably a part of the larger social totality, and that economic evolution therefore inevitably prepared the way for the evolution—or precipitated the revolution—of society. Whereas the Classicists had seen the "laws" of economic analysis as a means of predicting wages and prices and outputs, Marx saw them as a means of predicting social history.

And therein lay its deeper challenge. In effect Marxism was a return to a self-confident optimism not unlike that of Adam Smith—with, however, one critical difference: it was no longer capitalism which was thought to be the vehicle for the progress that history was inexorably enforcing. The forces of history were still the agents of human advance, but the price of that advance was now the abandonment of one social system for another.

This is not the place to enter into a critique of Marxist

thought. But there is one point about its optimism we must note. Insofar as it dealt with the immediate future, Marxism based its faith, as did the philosophy of Smith, on the belief that historic forces were the main cause of social change. But once the watershed of the socialist revolution had been passed, Marxian optimism no longer sought its reasons in the pressures of history. Thereafter Marxism launched into a Utopianism of its own. Compare Condorcet's dream of the Enlightenment:

> What a picture of the human race, freed from its chains, removed from the empire of chance as from that of the enemies of its progress, and advancing with a firm and sure step on the pathway of truth, of virtue, and of happiness. . . .[11]

with Engels' description of the consequences of the socialist revolution:

> The objective, external forces which have hitherto dominated history will then pass under the control of men themselves. It is only from this point that men, with full consciousness, will fashion their own history; it is only at this point that the social causes set in motion by men will have, predominantly and in constantly increasing measure, the effects willed by men. It is humanity's leap from the realm of necessity to the realm of freedom.[12]

[11] *Op. cit.*, Epoque X.
[12] F. Engels, "Anti-Dühring," from E. Burns, *Handbook of Marxism* (New York, 1935), p. 299.

9. *The End of European Optimism*

There will be ample opportunity in succeeding chapters to follow the historic consequences of that "leap into freedom." First we must quickly trace the main line of optimistic thought to the present.

What we have heretofore seen were but the initial evidences of a weakening European confidence in the forces of technology, democracy, and capitalist evolution. Yet in a century whose main historic sweep was one of vigorous expansion, the philosophy was by no means dealt a fatal blow. In America, as we shall see, optimism emerged unscathed from these miscarriages of hope. And even in Europe, well into the twentieth century something of the assured faith of the late eighteenth century remained. As Alfred Marshall, the greatest of the Victorian economists, wrote in the concluding pages of his *Principles of Economics*, in 1890, progress, "if slow is yet solid"; and in his last edition, in 1920, he saw no reason to alter the words.

Nonetheless there was a rising sense of unease. Although the philosophy of optimism remained the firmly held conviction of the Center, from both Left and Right it was subject to attack. On the one hand the social critics—Zola, Ibsen, Ruskin, Shaw—mocked at bourgeois conceptions of "progress" as little more than a rationale for getting rich. At the other extreme, the traditional aristocracy, which still comprised the core of conservative political thought, looked with something less than unrestrained enthusiasm upon a continuance of a trend that had already seriously jeopardized its privileges and status. Thus from the *avant-garde* progress was denounced as hypocrisy, while to the rear guard it was viewed as the entering wedge of revolution.

Meanwhile a deeper kind of disaffection was visible. Europe may have turned its face to the future but it could not entirely turn its back on a past that made itself visible in every cathedral and public monument. A sense of history which reached further back than the birth-years of the forces of progress imbued European thought with a characteristic bias—an awareness of profound secret problems of the human condition which neither technology nor democracy nor wealth could alleviate. For a while this "tragic" strain was subordinated to the enthusiasm of a century of great expectations. But by the turn of the century a change of mood was also visible: a *fin de siècle* weariness, a belated appreciation of the pessimism of Schopenhauer and the angry mysticism of Nietzsche. Later, when the debacle of the twentieth century was already in process, the tragic view of individual life and its collective history would find expression in such seminal works as Spengler's *Decline of the West*, Ortega y Gasset's *Revolt of the Masses*, Freud's *Civilization and Its Discontents*. To such minds the philosophy of optimism was but a thin gilding over the somber heritage of a forgotten past.

What ultimate effect these dissenting views might have had on the central core of optimism is a question whose answer we shall never know. For what happened in three decades of the twentieth century was a cataclysm of realities infinitely more powerful in changing men's attitudes than the mere erosion of ideas. From 1914 through 1945 Europe experienced a compression of horror without parallel in history: the carnage of the First World War, the exhaustion of the Depression, the agonizing descent of Germany into its fascist nightmare, the suicide of Spain, the humiliation of Italy, the French decay, the English decline—and finally the culminating fury of World War II. Before the cumulative tragedy of these years all optimistic views failed. Indeed the obvious question was no longer whether the forces of technology, democracy, and capitalism were the agents of a promising future, but the degree to which they should be held responsible for the unspeakably malevolent outcome of the past.

For certainly those forces could not be absolved of a major share in the blame for the European tragedy. The result of its technological "advance," for example, had been to change warfare from something still resembling human combat to a mechanized extermination process whose victims in two wars had exceeded fifty millions. As for the safeguarding forces of democracy, one could only note with incredulous dismay the supine acquiescence with which the masses of Germany and Italy had received—not to say welcomed—Caesarism. And, in the eyes of many, it had been the blind momentum of capitalism itself, which had brought on at least the first great war, and whose manifest malfunction was responsible for the insecurity and social disintegration that preceded the second.

But regardless of the blame one imputed to the forces of history for the past, the cataclysm of events worked a universal change in the estimation of these forces for the future. Even in peacetime, the development of mass technology had begun to suggest a trend of human deformation whose destination was unforgettably depicted in the sterile paradise of Huxley's *Brave New World*. Meanwhile the shattering experience of fascism had severely chastened the expectations of the supporters of democracy. George Orwell's *1984* was more than a ferocious caricature of dictatorship. It was also a forecast of a society which could no longer distinguish between enslavement and freedom—and worse yet, which no longer clearly preferred the latter to the former. Finally, the outlook for capitalism had lost most of its former assurance. When even its most buoyant reformer, John Maynard Keynes, could postulate the survival of the system only through its considerable socialization, a central pillar of the optimistic faith seemed to have collapsed.

Thus the legacy of the twentieth-century catastrophe in Europe has been a widespread acceptance of a pessimistic view of history's forces. An attitude which, but a few decades before, was confined to a dissenting minority of opinion has become the dominant philosophic and intellectual outlook. When we turn to contemporary European views of the future, we look in vain for the sustaining trust of the Victorian Age. This is not to say that contemporary European attitudes are marked with despair or that they evince a lack of courage. On the contrary, one finds stirring expressions of personal conviction and fortitude, and the European mood—at least on the surface—is resolute. What lacks is not *personal* optimism. It is *historic* optimism—that is, a belief in the imminence and immanence of change for the better in man's estate, the advent of which can be left to the quiet work of history.

Instead, at the very time when European material advance is exceeding all past performance, we find the dominant interpretations of history's currents tending not toward ideas of "progress" but in the direction of stasis or even decay. It is surely a commentary on the European outlook that its most acclaimed historian's *Study of History* should take for its theme "the process of the disintegrations of civilizations," or that the problem which should absorb so many European thinkers is the "absurdity" which destroys men's lives. There are no more confident expectations of inevitable progress at the hands of history in Europe today. There are only plans for survival.

It is true that in one part of Europe—the Soviet Union— an historic optimism continues to represent the dominant view of the future. But, ironically, it has been the very object lesson of Russia which has given the *coup de grâce* to the optimism of the rest of Europe. For, at least to an important group of European intellectuals, the Marxist transfer of optimism from capitalism to socialism was a sustaining hope amidst the catastrophes of their homelands. To them Russia was history incarnate, the living expression of those forces of progress which were elsewhere aborted by the social order in which they were confined. But when "humanity's leap from the realm of necessity to the realm of freedom" turned out to be a leap into a realm stricter, crueler, and more intellectually stifling than that of bourgeois capitalism, a kind of spiritual fatigue set in. The disillusion of the European Right and Center can be blamed on the terrible blows which assailed their plans for the present; but the disillusion of the European Left can only be blamed on the power of the blows which assailed its plans for the future.

10. *The American Experience*

Yet the rout of optimism in the twentieth century was not quite complete. If the belief in an automatically brightening future was vanquished by the harsh realities of events in Europe, in America something of the nineteenth-century faith remained. We have continued to trust in what the future "held out" for us. We have continued to be stubborn optimists.

Needless to say, we never consciously based this outlook on a calculated estimate of the prospects for historic change. On the contrary, we have always been convinced that the future would be propitious because we would *make* it so. Yet it must be clear by now that for all the naturalness and spontaneity of our self-assurance, behind it lay a tacit estimate of the forces of historic change. If we have had little doubt as to our ability to create a better world, it was because we have never questioned the kind of a world which was being created by the mass effects of scientific technology, by popular political aspiration, and by the dynamic inherent in our prevailing economic institutions. Thus when we said we were optimists, what we meant in fact was that we saw no conflict between our chosen goals and the flow of history's currents. Instead we saw each furthering the other.

To compare our continued trust in the future with the European mistrust in it is not merely to contrast differences of psychologies or of national characteristics. We need only reflect on the course of the European disillusion to recognize that our different expectations toward the future reflect different experiences with the past. For it is apparent that our exposure to history has not been that of Europe. To mention only the most obvious but centrally important fact, we have enjoyed a geographic isolation from history's assaults utterly unknown in Europe. No explanation of our persistent optimism can overlook the inexpressible importance of our ocean boundaries and weak neighbors as a cushion and buffer against history's blows. The ever-present threat of military conquest, the frictions of international coexistence at close quarters—these paramount realities of European history have, until the very recent past, played only a negligible role in our national consciousness.

Then too there must not be forgotten the equally unique advantage of our material independence. It has often been remarked that the American character was shaped by the presence of a huge and virtually uncontested continent, an enormous wealth of soil and ore and timber, a rugged but not impenetrable wilderness. Because the influence is well known does not mean that we can afford to lose sight of it. The abundance of nature has also been a circumstance of history which has markedly differentiated our expectations from those born in the more cramped environment of Europe.

A further cause of the optimistic mood which has always enthralled America must be sought in this nation's lack of an onerous past. If we have never displayed Europe's characteristic penchant for tragic thought, it is partly because we have never shared Europe's acquaintance with tragedy as an inseparable aspect of history. Unlike its mother-nations, America has never experienced the dragging weight of a changeless past; has never had to cope with the peasant tradition or with its resistance to change. In America we have no chastening ruins of past glories, no crumbling monuments to forgotten vanities. Of such pointed traces of the past, such counsels of futility, we have been as unencumbered as a people could be.

As a consequence, the same historic forces that we have followed in Europe took a very different turning here. In Europe, for example, the democratic movement brought with it an inheritance of social bitterness. On the one hand it grated on the sensibilities and the privileges of an entrenched aristocracy; on the other hand it was from the beginning a movement with an inexpungeable animus toward the past. In America there was no such social inheritance. From the outset American democracy was the *only* political movement of consequence, and therefore it developed in a mood of uncontested self-assurance. Hence when democracy in America, as in Europe, displayed its cultural and political shortcomings, it did not develop them in an atmosphere of tension, or with the possible consequences of total political upheaval or collapse. The historic force of democracy in America never displayed the face of *revolution* with which it was always uneasily associated abroad.

Again, in Europe the thrust of the new technology came upon a world already built, parceled out, stratified, and orderly. From the beginning the disruption caused by its mass industry was resisted or acquiesced in only fearfully—not alone by the old aristocracy but also by the newly arising laboring classes. In America, on the contrary, where patterns of society had not yet crystallized, the social disturbance brought about by the new industry was minimized. This is not to say that it did not exist, or that the growth of industry did not blight American cities and stunt American lives. It was rather that these side effects of technology did not impinge upon a community which was rooted with the tenacity of centuries in a division of labor and status inherited from the past. If technology upset American society, at least it upset a society which believed in mobility, and which trusted in change.

As a result the forces of technology and democracy were able to develop here with a minimum of fears and resistances from the past. In an atmosphere of general enthusiasm, their electrifying influences combined with our natural abundance to impart to American capitalism an *élan* very different from that of Europe. The only thought which accurately reflected the social and economic openness of America was *expansion*; the corresponding thought which matched the closed realities of Europe was that of *restraint*. While European capitalism was from the beginning socially defensive and economically constricted, capitalism in America was free of both rigidities of social structure and boundaries of economic horizons. Hence America planned and built on a gargantuan scale and its pace of advance was prodigious. Within fifty years of the death of Daniel Webster, our national wealth increased from less than a third that of Great Britain's to surpass it by more than a quarter. Our share of the world's total industrial production grew from insignificance in the beginning of the nineteenth century to over 20 per cent by 1860, and then to over 40 per cent by 1913.

Against this background of spectacular expansion, the fact that growth was uneven, attended by outrageous differentials between rich and poor, often wasteful and socially ruthless, simply did not matter—at least so far as our expectations were concerned. The accumulation of wealth on an unprecedented scale was the overriding reality of American history that carried all dissents and discontents before it.

And so, whereas we may have begun as optimists out of conviction, we remained so out of conditioning. For looking back over the special circumstances which favored our national career and which shaped our national character, we can see that we were spared the one exposure fatal to a philosophy of optimism. This was the experience which Europe suffered, first by small degrees, and then in overwhelming assault: an exposure to the forces of history not as the proponents but as the opponents of our volitions. Not only were we saved, by virtue of our geographic quarantine, from the impact of national wills other than our own, but by virtue of our clean historic slate we were spared the drag and friction of an enervating past. Thus circumstances conspired to give full rein to the historic forces at work in our midst, rather than, as in Europe, presenting them at every turn with obstacles and barriers. Democracy, technology, and capitalism all enjoyed an unobstructed course within the American environment, and all displayed a corresponding vitality of development.

Only once in our history, until the very recent past, did we find ourselves confronted with a situation in which these aspects of our national development seemed to run perversely and unaccountably counter to our expectations and efforts. This was the Great Depression. But the dazed perplexity which that experience aroused in us, the sense of incredulity that the Depression would not "cure itself," the extreme reluctance to believe that its cause might be rooted deep in the historic force of capitalist expansion—all this was testimony to the degree with which our experience with a benign past resulted in a fixity of expectations concerning the future.

H. G. Wells, writing on *The Future in America* in 1906, characterized the national temper as "a sort of optimistic fatalism." It was an apt observation. For as we strove to move in the very direction in which our social and political and economic drives propelled us and for which our geographic advantages fitted and protected us, we were never aware that our movement was due to any source other than the power of our wills, or that it might have any limitation other than our own aspirations. Still less did we entertain the idea that the forces of history might go *against* our volitions. As few peoples on earth, we were permitted the belief that we were the sole masters of our destiny, and as few peoples on earth have been, we were.

11.   *The Impasse of American Optimism*

It is precisely this sense of mastery of the past which finds it-self challenged so sharply by the present aspect of history. For the common attribute of contemporary events is not their responsiveness to our designs, but their indifference to them. Try as we will to steer our national course as we wish, we find our course being steered by events over which we seem to exert little if any control—the threat of nuclear war, or the chronic disorders of the newly aroused nations of the East and South, or the relentless pressure of communism, or simply the internal changes of our own society. History less and less presents itself as something we *make*, and more and more as something we find made for us. The mastery over our destiny, which has always been an unthinking assumption of our voyage into the hopeful future, now seems in danger of being wrested away by forces which neither precedent nor intuitive understanding illumines for us.

Yet, when we look more closely at the disturbing trends of current events, we find to our surprise that they are all familiar to us. One of them, which presents itself in the guise of the frightening technology of war, is of course the outgrowth of the scientific and technological development of the past. A second, which manifests itself as the revolutionary turbulence of the newly risen areas of the world, reflects nothing so much as the ideas of political aspiration that burst upon the world in 1789. A third, the global movement toward communism and socialism, can be seen also in the grand line of economic development whose early stages produced the capitalism of Adam Smith.

And so it is that when we seek to identify the currents of world history which now assail and defy us, we find ourselves ironically enough considering the very forces which, some three centuries ago, infused the future with hope and gave rise to the optimistic philosophy. Now, however, these forces have assumed a direction and dimension utterly unlike those of their appearance in our own history. It is obvious that the scientific and technological revolution has attained a momentum compared with which even our own past pace of technical progress appears as only a first stage of crude tooling-up. Certainly the ideas of political aspiration, planted among the billion and a half human beings who have until now existed in unspeakable poverty and neglect, will have a different outcome from the cultivation of those same ideas among the peoples of eighteenth-century Europe or our own nation. And equally clearly, the course of economic development takes on a wholly new guise when it is viewed in the context of a world which is now largely organized into non- or even anti-capitalist societies.

Thus if the origins of today's forces of historic change are familiar to us, their contemporary portents are very different from the era in which we have traced their influence. Cast in a wholly new setting, these forces are bringing about changes so vast, in a time span so compressed, and with adjustments so convulsive that it is as if huge seismic slippages were occurring in the deepest substratum of history. As this ponderous shifting of historic masses takes place, it is not surprising that the globe shakes, and that fissures open up beneath the strongest fortress walls.

Before these ominous developments of history, we react with the natural attitudes of our optimistic conditioning. If there are "forces" in history, we prefer not to think about them; and if we must think about them, we assume that they will be, as they always have been, on our side. As a result, while history has made mock of our plans, it has not weakened our confidence in our ability to shape our destiny as we wish. We are certain that the blame for the untoward drift of things can be laid at the doorstep of this President or that Congress. We continue to tell ourselves, in the face of successive rebuffs, that what we need above all is a fresh sense of purpose, a fresh idea of what to do. The one thought that does not enter our mind is that what we may more urgently need is a fresh sense of what to expect.

For it must be apparent that our philosophy of expectations is a parochial and sheltered one. The idea that there may be challenges in history which are irresistible, pitiless, unyielding; the thought that a people may often be not the masters but the prisoners of their time with no alternative but to bow before its demands; the intimation that there may sometimes be very little that a nation can do to bring about a state of world affairs or of domestic society which would approximate its desires—these are all conceptions about history which our optimism makes it extremely difficult for us to consider, much less accept.

Whether we shall have to accept these ideas is a matter to be considered in subsequent chapters. But what is already beyond doubt is that the essential nature of the American encounter with history is changing, and that our optimism is a handicap in appreciating that change and in assessing its implications. For our optimism blinds us to a central reality of our historic situation: that, after a long voyage in which the favoring currents of history bore us in the direction in which we sought to navigate, we have emerged into an open sea where powerful contrary winds come directly into conflict with our passage. To America—if not to Europe or to most of the rest of the world—this is an utterly new experience. It is as if history of a kind we had never known before were closing in upon us. We must try to understand what its portents for the future may be.

II

※

THE
CLOSING-IN
OF
HISTORY

1. *The Impact of the Bomb*

Heretofore we have been interested in the forces of history insofar as they conditioned our expectations concerning the future. Now we must come to grips with them, not in an abstract context, but as tangible realities which are visibly shaping the environment of tomorrow. We must search among the specific challenges of our time for evidence of the larger patterns of our historic situation.

When we then turn to these specific challenges, there is no doubt as to which one first draws our attention. This is the towering threat of the new technology of war. If any single happening of our age has made its impact felt upon this nation, it is the prospect of mass destruction to which we are now exposed.

The general characteristics of that prospect are so well known as to require only the briefest mention. A subcommittee of the Joint Congressional Committee on Atomic Energy has predicted the result of an attack in which 224 military and civilian targets would be hit by 263 hydrogen bombs. In the ensuing explosions (equal to 1,446,000,000 tons of TNT), about 23,000,000 people would be killed immediately. Another

25,900,000 would be so badly injured that they would subsequently die. Thus by a single blow the new technology could produce an American death roll equal to that suffered by *all* participants in ten years of two World Wars.

This is so huge a disaster that it becomes almost impossible to view it without statistical remoteness. The horror of the catastrophe becomes more meaningful when we narrow our focus to a single disaster, such as that which could be produced by dropping a megaton weapon into the Hudson River. In itself this could create a tidal wave big enough to drown most of the inhabitants of Manhattan.[1]

It is clear that this terrifying prospect presents America with an unprecedented need to revise its outlook for the future. With brutal abruptness the new war technology has knocked out the keystone of our optimistic philosophy by forcing us to confront the possibility of national extinction, an eventuality which has never before even remotely entered our calculations. As no other development of our age, the nuclear threat has torn down the barriers which have held "history" at a remove from the American consciousness.

And yet when we go beyond these rather obvious considerations, we can see that the new war technology has other and more tangible consequences than the supreme degree of risk it poses. For the new weaponry presents not alone a threat for the future, but a changed objective reality for the present. Whether or not the weapons of total destruction are ever put to their "intended" use, their very existence alters our history-

[1] *New York Times*, July 23, 1958. Statement by Lieutenant General Clarence Huebner, director of the New York State Civil Defense Commission

making possibilities in a number of profoundly important ways.

The first of these is rather paradoxical. It is that the most formidable advance ever made in the science of warfare has as its immediate result not the enhancement but the *diminution* of the traditional power of military force on history. This state of affairs comes about, of course, as a consequence of the change in the nature of war itself. Formerly the cost of an unsuccessful military venture was usually no more than a military defeat. Today, since an all-out attack would almost certainly trigger an all-out response, the cost of even a "successful" military attack is likely to be a return of fire heavy enough to produce social collapse. Because such a suicidal course cannot recommend itself to any nation except as a policy *in extremis*, the categorical imperative of military conduct therefore becomes to *avoid* pressing an atomically armed enemy into a situation of total desperation, rather than to seek for "victory" at all costs.[2] Two powers facing one another with a full panoply of nuclear missiles thus come more and more to resemble the cumbrously armored knights of the Middle Ages who, fearsomely accoutered for war, were hindered by their armaments from waging it effectively.

This is not to say, as we know from contemporary history, that *less* than all-out military force no longer has its impact on the course of events. Nor is it to conclude dogmatically that all-out war is "impossible." The point is, rather, that in a critical collision of national aims between atomic powers

[2] See H. Kissinger, *Nuclear Weapons and Foreign Policy* (New York, 1957).

military force alone cannot any longer ensure its *traditional* conclusion for either side. The basic function of the military —to achieve victory over the enemy—has been rendered obsolete by the fact that "victory" and defeat are almost certain to be achieved simultaneously.

What we find, then, is that the potential direct history-making power of the new military weapons has been considerably neutralized by the technological characteristics of those weapons. It is more than likely, for example, that were nuclear weapons to be effectively barred by an atomic disarmament conference, and the ultimate catastrophe thus banished, the chances of large-scale war would be considerably strengthened. Strangely, we reach the conclusion that whereas nuclear weaponry offers us a greater power for "heroic" history-making than ever before—while it literally possesses us of the thunderbolts of Zeus—so long as we are afraid to use those thunderbolts, it only opens the future wider to the influence of the non-heroic determinants of history.

All this, of course, has a direct relevance to our great contest with Russia. The technology of war makes it impossible to contemplate the "elimination" by force of Russia or, what is more important, of communism. That convenient solution of the past, which was effective as late as World War II as a means of disposing of fascism, is simply no longer at hand. Our "coexistence" with Russia and with communism is in no sense a matter of rational political "choice," but is at bottom a necessity imposed by technological realities.

Second, the self-defeating destructiveness of total nuclear war throws the determination of our contest of ideologies and world influence to the gradual erosion of ideas, the slow pressures of economics, or the virtuosity of political leadership. The greatest of all military weapons has thus plunged us more directly than ever into the mainstream of the historic currents of our day.

2.   The Impact of the Machinery of War

But this is by no means the full historic impact of the new war technology. Indeed, the very inconclusiveness of what we have hitherto seen suggests that our angle of approach has been too narrow. We have been attempting to examine the nuclear apparatus as a *weapon*. Now we must examine it in its more basic aspect as a *machine*.

It is, of course, an enormously complicated machine whose "parts" include hundreds of factories, launching sites, laboratories, storage depots, and the like. But the very complexity of its technology gives us an insight into its historic ramifications. We would expect a machine of such huge proportions to require a very large body of men to tend it. And this is precisely what we find. The new technology of war may be singularly ineffective as an instrument of national policy, but it has brought about a considerable increase in the power and position of its keepers—the military.

It is curious how little this fact has been remarked upon. Few descriptions of the contemporary American scene place much emphasis on our military organization as the most decisively contrasting aspect of our society today with that of the past. We often talk about the change in the position of "government," "business," or "labor" over the past twenty years, but rarely about the change in our degree of militarization. Yet in numbers, power, influence, or social status there has been no more impressive shift between the pre-aerial and atomic and the post-aerial and atomic ages. Today the Department of Defense and its subordinate branches employ a larger number of civilian workers than the entire federal government of a generation ago. Since the end of World War II, direct military expenditures (*excluding* veterans' affairs) have never been less than a third of the federal budget and have risen to nearly seventy per cent in recent years.[3] Meanwhile our military apparatus is responsible, through its procurement operations, for purchasing a tenth of our entire Gross National Product, a proportion which some expect to grow to a seventh during the next twenty years.[4] In addition, the military not only supports by far the largest science establishment in the nation, but its financial contributions to some universities for research far exceed their receipts from any other source. And perhaps most important of all is the extraordinary elevation in position and prestige of the military in the general public estimation. Amid the general esteem surrounding the armed forces today, it is difficult to recall that only twenty years ago

[3] *Statistical Abstract* (1956), table 277, p. 234.
[4] Committee for Economic Development, *Problems of United States Economic Development* (New York, 1958), vol. I, p. 29, essay by Dr. Simon Kuznets.

Americans were known for and prided themselves on their distaste for and distrust of everything military.

This rise in the power and prestige of the military is not a reflection of an increased appetite for war. It is brought about simply by the fact that the new machinery of war requires a larger number of workers to tend it. "It is an illusion," writes George Fielding Eliot, "to suppose . . . that more powerful and complex weapons make possible a reduction in military man-power—all experience indicates the exact contrary. Thus a recent Pentagon study shows that the delivery of a given weapons-yield by means of missiles to a given distance requires more man-power, not less, than an equivalent delivery by manned aircraft."[5]

But there is as well a second technological reason for the growth of military power. As we have seen, the all-or-nothing character of total nuclear warfare leads to a kind of muscle-bound impotence for a nation possessed *only* of the armament of nuclear weapons. Hence if military power is to be made usable, particularly in small increments, the giant weapon of thermonuclear striking power must be supplemented by a full spectrum of the more conventional types of arms. Not one, but at least two levels of full war capability are concurrently demanded.

Furthermore, this multi-tiered capability of military action must be maintained in a condition of readiness never heretofore contemplated. Nuclear capabilities cannot wait on a leisurely industrial mobilization if they are to serve as a valid psychological or physical threat. It is only the nuclear power "in being" —not that in the laboratory or even in production—which

[5] *Ibid.*, p. 371.

counts as effective strength. Since our all-out capabilities of attack or of retaliatory defense can be no more than the explosive power we can deliver in a matter of hours, a huge armamentarium must be kept in a state of constant readiness. But so too must the subsidiary forces which fight under the shadow of a leashed atomic power. If small wars are to be fought effectively, and thus prevented from gaining the dangerous momentum of big wars, well-equipped expeditionary forces must be brought to bear within a matter of days. Thus the exigencies of limited as well as of all-out war necessitate a strong and permanent military installation.

It is possible, of course, that a political *détente* may gradually lessen the importance which now attaches to military capabilities. But even a considerable relaxation of tension will hardly permit us to return to the pre-atomic subordination of military affairs. As we shall have cause to see, even without the presence of the Soviet Union, the world will be an exceedingly dangerous place to live in over the foreseeable future. The outbreak of small wars is virtually a certainty, and some of these will have the potential to develop into large wars. The likely extension of nuclear armaments to secondary powers in the near future, and possibly to tertiary powers in the not too distant future, will all add uncertainty and risk to the prospects for international history. Thus it is extremely unlikely under the best of circumstances that we shall permit our highly trained cadres of professionals in nuclear or conventional war to dissipate their skills, their organization, their effectiveness. Nor is it likely that we would allow the facilities for the production of war goods to remain unused, or even unbuilt. The position of high importance, prestige, and sheer magnitude of organization which the military now occupy in *every* atomically armed industrial power must be regarded as a historic result of the impact of the new technology of war upon modern society.

That such a prospect raises grave questions of a political and social kind, especially for a democratic society, need hardly be emphasized. The pre-eminence accorded the military in the determination of affairs of state cannot but raise uneasy feelings that what C. Wright Mills calls "the military metaphysic" may become the prevailing interpretation of world history. So too the steady extension of business dependence upon the military subeconomy, and the equally steady conversion of so much scientific and intellectual effort into a parasitic outgrowth of military research tends to bring support for military programs from these important (and traditionally antimilitary) groups. Finally it must not be lost to sight that only during the eighteenth and nineteenth centuries, when the future was entrusted to the benign determinism of history, was the military generally relegated to a position of quasi-civil service obedience to the civil authorities. Previously, when history was conceived and executed in terms of heroic endeavors, the military naturally provided the core of social order. Hence if the contemporary forces of history gather strength and display unruly tendencies, it would not be surprising if once again the military moved into a more active political role.

To be sure, we must guard against misleading stereotypes of the past. The traditional concept of "militarism" describes an ideology and a social type which the new technology itself is fast rendering obsolete. The military man today is more aptly characterized as "technician," "administrator," or simply "bureaucrat" than as "soldier." On the whole, contemporary military thinking tends to be more sober in tone, more realistically appreciative and apprehensive of the consequences of large-scale war, than some of that emanating from the supposedly more peaceably inclined civil branches of government. Certainly it is more circumspect than the aggressive promptings of chauvinist or proto-fascist groups within the nation at large. In a word, the "military mind" is less readily distinguishable from the prevailing "responsible" views of society than was perhaps once the case.

Thus it would be rash to jump to conclusions about the political consequences of the ascendant military power. It is enough to recognize that its power is in the ascendant, bringing with it an inescapable increase in the hierarchies, the large bureaucracies, the organizational massiveness by which a military machine is characterized. Whether that growing social machine will threaten a democratic society we do not know. That it will be a permanent addition to it is a likelihood which we must be prepared to face.

3. *The Social Machine*

And it is only now that we touch on the ultimate historic effect of the new weaponry. It lies in the realization that the final impact of all technology is to be found in the *social organization* which it calls forth.

Our age tends to picture the impact of the science and technology to which it has so willingly surrendered as consisting only in a dazzling stream of new machines, new processes, new "miracles" of technical performance. Hence we do not see that it is not alone, or even primarily, the mechanisms of science and technology which leave their imprint on our times. It is the unadvertised, and often the inadvertent, *social consequences* of those mechanisms. Science appeals to us as the means whereby we gain control over our environment. What we fail to notice is that it also forges a new social environment with formidable powers of control over us.

The powerful social repercussions of nuclear weaponry—all the more impressive in that the physical machinery itself has not been put to "use"—thereby serve as a paradigm of the general impact of science and technology. They direct our attention to the extent to which the unintentional social by-products of science and technology can come to overshadow in importance the material accomplishments which alone are intended. These material accomplishments enable us to control powerful processes of nature, to voyage without thought of distance, to speak to and listen to voices a thousand miles away, to build and enjoy extraordinary mechanisms which "enrich" our lives in one way or another. Yet to this generally recognized end-product of science and technology must be added a second end-product which also springs from the ubiquitous presence of our machines. The enormous and now cancerous cities in which we live, the size and impersonality of the offices and factories in which we work, the intimate exposure to the prevailing culture from which we cannot escape, the ceaseless refashioning of the "standards" by which our lives are self-evaluated, the very "complexity" of life before which we experience a sinking impotence—these are also characteristics of modern existence whose source can be traced in large part to the environment which science and technics create in our midst.

Perhaps the most impressive instance of the controlling environment which science forges for us is the industrial process itself. There is now a large and eloquent literature on the pressures exerted by industrial technology upon its human "masters." The assembly line and the office have both received increasing attention as human environments whose psychological demands are as great as the physiological demands of the natural environment which they have displaced. It is today only a commonplace to point out what Adam Smith first noticed: that in the process of industrialization we find ever more refined, and complexly interrelated operations requiring of their operatives ever lower contributions of spontaneous and creative work. "Technical progress," concludes Suzanne K. Langer, "is putting man's freedom of mind into jeopardy."[6]

The process of technological control and conditioning extends far beyond the bounds of factory and office, however. Indeed, it invades life to a degree which is so pervasive and diffuse that few of us are any longer consciously aware of it. As Dr. Langer eloquently describes one aspect of it:

> The ordinary city-dweller knows nothing of the earth's productivity; he does not know the sunrise and rarely notices when the sun sets; ask him what phase the moon is in, or when the tide in the harbor is high, or even how high the average tide runs, and likely as not he cannot answer you. Seed time and harvest are nothing to him. If he has never witnessed an earthquake, a great flood or a hurricane, he probably does not feel the power of nature as a reality surrounding his life at all. His realities are the motors that run elevators, subway trains, and cars, the steady feed of water and gas through the mains and of electricity over the wires, the crates of food-stuff that arrive by night and are spread for his inspection before his day begins, the concrete and brick, bright steel and dingy woodwork that take the place of earth and waterside and sheltering roof for him. . . . Nature, as man has always known it, he knows no more.[7]

Instead he knows society. But this "society" is not the interplay of intimates, but the impersonal articulation of millions

[6] *Philosophy in a New Key* (Mentor ed., 1951), p. 238. See also Hannah Arendt, *The Human Condition* (Chicago, 1958); Daniel Bell, *Work and Its Discontents* (Boston, 1956); Walker & Guest, *The Man on the Assembly Line* (Cambridge, 1952).

[7] *Philosophy in a New Key*, p. 226.

of strangers into a working whole. It is the creation of an environment in which human beings "function" as parts of an elaborate social machine, and in which there are ever fewer aspects of life which do not involve the co-operative effort of other human beings.

This does not mean that science and technology destroy the individual or that they empty his life or that they do not equip him with unimaginable powers. It is not to decry the effects of penicillin, jet planes, automatic kitchens, or electronic communication that we call attention to their social impact. It is only to make clear that these technical advances create a new environment for man, and furthermore an environment which, although man-made, is as demanding, incomprehensible, even arbitrary as the environment of nature. Man is now as much at the mercy of his own artifacts as ever he was impotent before the winds and seasons. But whereas man made his peace with nature very largely as an individual—as a farmer, a hunter, a fisherman, a sailor—he makes his peace with technology through social organization. The technology itself demands organization in order to function, and the environment it creates in turn calls forth organization in order for men to function within it. Thus we find that the incursion of science and technology creates an ever-higher order of *social control*, partly visible in the hierarchies of the huge productive firms, partly in the corresponding hierarchies of public institutions which co-ordinate, restrain, and buffer their operations. Meanwhile, as their invisible companion, there proceeds as well the psychological "socialization" of the individual—his steadily enforced conception of himself as part of a huge and impersonal social machine.

The fact that an invention as remote from "life" as the nuclear bomb calls forth an added degree of social organization in our midst alerts us to the ubiquity of this phenomenon. Even the most "unhistoric-minded" person sees in science a means by which the future will be shaped. But what so many of the strongest proponents of science do not understand is that along with its advance also goes an advance in the complexity of our social organization. In our next chapter we shall return again to this question. At this juncture it is enough to see in the socializing influence of science and technology one of the forces which are closing in on the American future, shaping for it an historic environment whose attributes may not be of our conscious making.

4. The Awakening of the Colonial World

We have thus far been concerned with the effect which science in general and the new weapons technology in particular have had and will continue to have on our future. Now we must turn to the second of the great historic currents of our times. This is the revolutionary extension of popular political aspiration to the underdeveloped world.

At its roots the basic motivation of the contemporary revolution is a diffuse phenomenon. It is a movement of the "popular will" which springs from the awakening, in many millions of minds, of ideas of dignity, hope, ambition. But in the actualities of history we do not encounter it in such spiritual dress. Instead we meet it as an aspect of contemporary events with which we are very familiar under another guise—that of the increased turbulence of the "new" political areas of the world.

We need only to be reminded of a few instances of this characteristic "troublesomeness" of the underdeveloped nations. We find it in a movement away from constitutional government toward authoritarian and often militaristic regimes in many backward nations, including many of those nominally a part of the "Free World." We see it in the prevalence of local international tensions which result in an Indian-Pakistan rift, an Egyptian-Israeli war. We meet it again in the instability of governments which manifests itself in assassinations in Guatemala, Iraq; civil wars in Cuba, Indonesia; revolutionary turmoil in Algeria, riots in the Belgian Congo. And most important of all, we encounter it as an economic movement leftward which can be seen to some degree in nearly all the new nations.

It is difficult at first to connect this diversity of troubles with the rise and spread of the idea of political aspiration. And yet when we place these occurrences in an historic perspective, we can see that they have an integral connection with that revolution of expectations whose appearance in Europe in the eighteenth century contributed so much to our own changed attitude toward the future. Only, what is now happening is an extension of that essentially restricted revolution on a world-wide scale.

For we must realize that the seemingly vast industrial, political, and economic changes which ushered in modern history were in fact a series of events that directly affected only a tiny fraction of the world's population. Whole continents, entire cultures, vast societies were left aside in their course. Indeed, for the overwhelming majority of the world's people the revolution simply did not exist. Technologically, the bulk of the peoples on the Eurasian, Asiatic, African, and South American land-masses remained in a pre-industrial and even a neolithic stage of development. Politically they continued to exist as a voiceless serfdom, which was generally the only condition of political existence they had ever known. Economically, although millions lay under the formal sovereignty of capitalist nations, only a fringe had any personal involvement in their Western ways of life.

For the last three centuries, in other words, there existed side by side two nearly separate worlds. One, mainly comprising the people of Europe and North America, was the beneficiary of the multiform revolution which had slowly come to maturity in its midst. The other, comprising the peoples of East and South, was its victim. For the contact between the two worlds, although restricted, was highly infectious. Indeed, it was toxic.

In part this was because the small and active European civilization often ruthlessly exploited the large and torpid Asiatic and African ones. Predatory as it was, however, this economic exploitation was perhaps the *least* destructive aspect of imperialism. In a sense it was only an intensified transplanting of an attitude toward labor which was also visible within the Western community. What was much more disastrous for the colonial world was that its economic penetra-

tion by the West came without any of the historic preparation that accompanied this development in Europe. Imperialism
imposed on its colonies the raw economic drive of capitalism
without the social and political underpinnings and protec-
tions which blunted that drive at home.

The result was in many ways a catastrophe for the colonial
world. Into its primitive circulation of life a powerful and
dangerous virus was injected with terrible effect. It turned
millions of traditionally self-sufficient peasants into rubber-
tappers, coffee-growers, tin-miners, tea-pickers—and then sub-
jected this new agricultural and mining proletariat to the incomprehensible vagaries of world commodity fluctuations.
It uprooted ancient laws and gave in exchange Western justice,
whose ideas disrupted the local culture by striking at the roots
of time-honored traditions and customs. It brought young men
to the universities of Europe to learn the thought of the West,
and then placed them in jail when they went home to preach
it. Immense strides were made in orderly government, but it
was government over and not of the people, and almost in-
variably concerned with preserving the prerogatives of feudal
overlords rather than extending new privileges to the masses
beneath them. Colonialism, even in its most missionary moments, never succeeded in seeing the "natives" as equals, and it
usually simply took for granted their irremediable inferiority.

It is useless to lament this tragic chapter of the past, and
still less useful to exaggerate its horrors. While colonialism was
economically, socially, and politically disrupting and disturbing, one cannot forget that the way of life which it displaced
was often brutally cruel and tyrannical. Nor can one ignore
the gains which came with the penetration of the West: health

and sanitation, transport and communication, law and order, and not least, the necessary stimulation to waken torpid peoples from their enslavement to the past.

But whereas the historic role of colonialism was a complex one, it is essential to recognize that the historic condition which produced it has now come to an end. The coexistence of two worlds, one active, one passive, is everywhere disappearing or has already vanished. With enormous rapidity the transformation of history which three centuries ago began to reorient the internal direction of Western man is now reorienting the face of man throughout the world. Attitudes of despair and futility, so deeply engrained that they manifested themselves not as frustration but as indifference, have given way to a new sense of impatience, desire, hope. The revolutionary concept of a meaningful future—of social progress —has finally penetrated to those vast areas of the world which until just recently existed silently and inertly alongside the ferment of the West. And with this change in attitude toward the future, there are being brought about not only the most rapid readjustments in world events, but—with the rising up of the new continents—the very inception of historic change on a truly world scale.

5. *The Terrible Ascent*

In its ultimate implications this is perhaps the most important revolution which mankind has ever experienced. Its eventual beneficiaries number more than a billion and a half human beings who are today the *misérables* of the earth.

Yet if their awakening from an agelong slumber marks the turning of a new page for humanity, it is also the commencement of a chapter of tragedy and sorrow. For the metamorphosis from poverty into decency will be a struggle of Herculean proportions and Sisyphian discouragement. Far from leading in a gradual progression toward enlightenment and well-being, it is almost certain to result at first in increased misery, violence, and unrest.

Typically a country which is now entering the mainstream of world history displays a schizophrenic attitude toward the world. In part it nurses its bitter memories of the past; in part it reaches for the future with a naïve enthusiasm. Hopefully and under good leadership, the latter attitude may come to predominate. But corresponding to this energizing shift of mind cannot come a commensurate mobilization of resources. What hinders the advance to the new future is not, so to speak, the lack of an automobile. It is not even the lack of shoes. It is the lack of a road.

Merely to highlight this terrible absence of the wherewithal for advance, let us contrast that most basic resource—power—in India and the United States. In India, in 1953, man and beast produced 65 per cent of all the nation's economic energy, and of the remaining 35 per cent of inanimately produced power almost three-quarters was secured by the burning of dung.[8] In the United States human and animal power together accounted for but one per cent of the nation's economic energy, and the use of primitive animal fuels was zero. As a consequence, India's total electric power supply was only about one-fiftieth of America's, and, on a per-capita basis, less than half of that. The total amount of electric power generated by India would not suffice to light up New York City.

To this typical and crippling lack of power—a lack which can be duplicated in industrial requirements of every description—must be added the further handicap of an absence of the institutions needed for its repair. Nothing like a "capital market" to mobilize savings exists in most underdeveloped nations. Chronic shortages of foreign exchange restrict their import programs to a minimum. And perhaps most crippling of all is a lack of adequate *human* resources: workmen who can read and who understand the rhythms of industrial production, businessmen whose attitude toward business is to produce rather than to gouge, specialists of every variety, government officials who can transcend a tradition of bureaucratic indifference and petty graft. In a word, such societies

[8] Wit and Clubok, "Atomic Power Development in India," *Social Research*, Autumn, 1958, p. 290.

tend to lack an "economic" population. They are made up of peasants rather than farmers, laborers rather than workers, peddlers and speculators rather than managers, sinecurists rather than government administrators. To be sure, this condition of economic backwardness varies considerably from, say, Mexico, to colonial Africa. But in general outline these maladies of underdevelopment are visible and vitiating in all.

Under these conditions there is only one way in which a massive and rapid economic advance can be begun, much less carried through. It must be done from the top. When men do not know what to do, when by habit they do the wrong things, when they do not understand the signals of the market place, or when this market place does not yet exist, then men must be told what to do. Every emergent nation, in beating its way to progress, must adopt a greater or lesser degree of centralized control over its economy, and the lower down on the scale is its starting point, the greater does that degree of control tend to be.

Thus we find a degree of collectivism vigorously espoused by nearly every underdeveloped nation—sometimes, as in Pakistan or Egypt, of a nationalist military complexion; sometimes, as with India, Indonesia, Ghana, of socialist leanings. No doubt the ideological preferences of their leaders play a role in this general collectivist orientation. Their bitter past experience with *laissez faire*, their disbelief in the willingness of the capitalist West, even now, to mount a really major effort of economic assistance, their susceptibility to Marxian optimism —all these factors play their roles. Yet at bottom the appeal of collectivism is not intellectual or emotional. It is functional.

For even if the backward nations wished to develop under

the aegis of capitalism, capitalism is not so easily achieved. It rests on inner motivations, inner disciplines, on learned habits of economic "rationality" which cannot be inculcated into a peasant population overnight. In England it took generations before the uprooted yeomanry stopped burning down the factories they despised. In Prussia, Frederick the Great used to complain that his merchants were so timid and unventuresome that he had to drag them to their profits "by their noses and ears." Thus capitalism must grow up slowly, out of the experience of generations—and it is even doubtful in today's world if it would grow at all. Certainly it cannot be imposed, full-blown. But collectivism can. Peasants, money-lenders, petty bureaucrats can be told—ordered—to do what must be done. As a means of beginning the huge transformation of a society, an economic authoritarian command has every advantage over the incentives of enterprise.

Hence the very least that one can expect of the new economies is a powerful and prominent degree of central direction and control within a "free enterprise" milieu. But the logic of events does not stop with this arrangement. On the contrary, in the setting of underdevelopment, powerful forces are likely to press "mixed economies" in the direction of political and economic extremes.

For the enthusiasm of the initial awakening of a people soon outruns the reality of its sluggish progress. No matter how heroic the efforts of its regime, no underdeveloped nation can hope to make headway quickly. Indeed the fearsome possibility is that at first its condition may deteriorate. The early stages of the new industrialization will only add to the social dislocation which began under colonialism. The initial heavy investments will weigh upon rather than uplift the general population. Not least, the pressures of population growth, which are the main enemy of progress in nearly every under-developed land, will grow worse as broad health and sanitation measures take effect.

Thus the road to progress may well be more terrible than the roadless and mindless existence of the past. Nevertheless, once the great march has begun, it is no longer possible to turn back. The changes in the balance of the old static society cannot be undone. There is no choice but to tread the road to its conclusion—however long and agonizing the journey may be.

We need only think of the seventy-five to one hundred years which elapsed in Europe before industrialism began to make known its benefits, to understand the dismal prospect which stretches before every peasant nation, scratching its way up the cliff with its fingernails. In most of Asia, for example, the per-capita standard of living of the population is represented as "less than $100 a year." This is a standard which in fact defies numerical treatment: it means existence at the borderline of animal needs. If the pace of economic growth in Asia now continues at about its present rate, and if the Asiatic nations begin to control their population floods, it is possible that these per-capita "standards" may be boosted by 2 per cent a year. The peasants and city masses of the East can therefore look forward to the prospect that by the year 2000 their incomes may have reached a level of $200 a year. This is well below the level now "enjoyed" by a Portuguese peasant or by a farmer in the poverty-stricken lands of southern Italy.

After forty years of immense labors, the result will still be abysmal poverty.

Thus economic development, in its agonizing slow pace, will not give rise to a glad acquiescence in the future and a sense of relief that progress is now on the march. On the contrary, every step forward is apt to worsen the mood of disaffection, to stir the fires of impatience. Economic development in its early stages is not a process of alleviating discontent. Initially it is the cause of deepening it.

6. The "Leap into Freedom"

Needless to say, all this lends a dark color to the outlook for a mild economic transition. High hopes, once aroused, are not so easily retired, and a government which does not satisfy the aspirations on which it rides into power will soon give way to another which will promise to do more.

This leads to two likely prospects. The first is the rise of authoritarian regimes in the underdeveloped nations. For the capacity for action of parliamentary governments is apt to prove inadequate to the heroic demands of rapid development. Parliamentary governments, even in those rare cases where they do not merely represent the privileged classes of peasant nations, naturally act to *slow down* the pace of social change by seeking to accommodate minority interests—a function which may be highly desirable once a level of tolerable social satisfaction has been reached, but hardly one which is apt to commend itself to a newly aroused and highly dissatisfied people.

Even in Western governments, built upon fairly stable social foundations, we have seen how vulnerable and weak are parliamentary regimes in times of stress, unless they produce their own "strong men"—as witness the cases of pre-Mussolini Italy and pre-Hitler Germany, of republican Spain and postwar France. Among the underdeveloped nations, bereft of any tradition of democratic compromise and cohesion, this tendency is a thousandfold multiplied. Thus we find the emergence of the soldier-ruler: in Pakistan, in Egypt, in China, in Burma, in Taiwan, in the succession of Latin-American junta governments. And while this array clearly reveals that not every authoritarian government is itself an agency for economic transformation, it stands to reason that, with the added stresses and strains of rapid development, the "attractions" of authority are made all the greater.

But the second prospect is even more sobering. It is the likelihood that the predominant authoritarianism will veer increasingly to the extreme Left.

For in their situations of genuine frustration, one lesson will not be lost upon the underdeveloped nations. This is the fact that two peasant countries in the twentieth century have succeeded in making the convulsive total social effort which alone seems capable of breaking through the thousand barriers of scarcity, ineptitude, indifference, inertia. These are the Soviet Union and now, even more impressively, China. It might be objected that the underdeveloped nations could also fasten their gaze on other nations, such as Western Germany or Japan, which have also recently shown startling rates of growth. But these are nations with their initial industrial "transformations" behind them. They began where the underdeveloped regions now seek to arrive. Russia to a considerable degree and China even more unmistakably began at scratch.

We are only beginning to appreciate the magnitude of the Chinese effort. Until recently we have been so repelled by the severity of the Chinese communist methods, with their Spartan communes, that we have overlooked what is the most significant fact about these methods. This is the attainment of what seems to be by far the largest rate of economic growth ever achieved by any peasant nation. According to the best estimates we now have (which discount China's own extravagant claims), China's per-capita output has been growing since 1952 at a rate of over 6 per cent a year.[9] This is a pace of advance which is between *double* and *triple* the rate of growth thus far achieved by India under non-collectivist conditions.

Meanwhile an equally startling performance has been evinced by the Soviet Union. Until the present decade of world history, the generally accepted paragon of economic progress was the United States. This is no longer true. Mr. Allen W. Dulles, comparing our performance with the Soviets, has noted:

[9] A. Doak Barnett, *Communist Economic Strategy: The Rise of Mainland China* (National Planning Association, 1959), table 2. See also William V. Hollister, *Chinese Gross National Product and Social Accounts, 1950-1957* (Illinois, 1958); and Wilfred Malenbaum, "India and China: Contrasts in Development Performance," *American Economic Review*, June, 1959.

> Whereas Soviet gross national product was about 35 percent of that of the United States in 1950 . . . by 1962 it may be about 50 percent of our own. This means that the Soviet economy has been growing and is expected to grow through 1962 at a rate roughly twice that of the economy of the United States.[10]

To be sure, what strikes us in considering both instances of economic growth is the immense human price which has been paid for material progress. The social agonies of development—the use of forced labor, mass executions, the bludgeoning of the peasant into collectives and the Stakhanovist methods of securing industrial discipline—these are well known. In the case of China, the human cost is even more nakedly revealed in the use of human labor as "capital." Essentially China has achieved its startling increases in output—in the case of food, a tripling of crops since 1949; in the case of steel, a sevenfold increase in the same period—by massively applying organized human effort in the same fashion and with the same huge end results as the Pharaohs used in constructing the pyramids.

Yet what seems to us to be a fearful exaction in terms of human suffering, political outrage, and slave labor conditions may not appear so intolerable to peoples who have always suffered, never known political freedom, and labored all their lives and all their histories as serfs. Human "price" is, after all, a matter of alternatives, and in the eyes of the underdeveloped peoples the alternatives do not allow for nice calculations of "comfort" and "austerity." Rather the choice is between a violent and often frightfully costly effort for a generation or

[10] *New York Times,* April 29, 1958.

two in the hope of freeing future generations from the yoke, or the patient endurance of a now bitterly resented misery for many generations while a more humane, but far slower, transformation is achieved.

There is no blinking the arduousness of this choice. Even existence at the very margin of life can be worsened by the extreme efforts of an all-out development drive, for people at the margin of existence can be driven over that margin into premature death. But this hideous price must be weighed against a continuation of the present state of affairs. In this truly anguishing choice, our own preferences for gradualism may well reflect nothing but our inability to appreciate the intolerable condition of life as it now exists in much of the world. Looking at the alternatives from below rather than from above, it is understandable that it may not be the *price* but the *promise* of rapid advance which exerts the more powerful sway. As the late John Foster Dulles has written: "We can talk eloquently about liberty and freedom, and about human rights and individual freedoms, and about the dignity and worth of the human personality, but most of our vocabulary derives from a period when our own society was individualistic. Consequently it has little meaning to those who live under conditions where individualism means early death."[11]

It would be both foolish and dangerous to maintain that all underdeveloped countries "must" sooner or later succumb to a rigorous communist collectivism in order to effect a major economic advance. Between one backward nation and another there are vast differences in needs, resolves, resources. One cannot easily generalize over a spectrum that includes

[11] *War or Peace* (New York, 1950), p. 257.

such different cases as Brazil and Burma, Libya and Turkey. In many of the backward nations the critical determining factor may be the "historic force" of a commanding, but democratic and gradualist figure, such as a Nehru or a Muñoz Marin.

But honesty compels us to admit that Nehrus and Muñoz Marins are rare and still more rarely succeed one another, and that behind striking national differences is a common desire for advance which, once fanned, grows hotter and more impatient. Taking the long perspective of the decades ahead, it is difficult to ignore the relative "efficiency" of authoritarian over parliamentary regimes as a means of inaugurating growth, or the truly remarkable growth rates which, thus far at least, have only been attainable under the radical social reorganization of communist collectivism. Nor can one ignore the fact that property relations, as they now exist in many underdeveloped nations, often serve to impede the needed mobilization of resources even more than they facilitate it; and that the direction in which property institutions guide new capital may not be that which is most critically required for the future. All these facts must inevitably exert their gravitational pull on the course of events, and when we weigh their relative attractive powers it seems hard to doubt in which direction the compass needle of development will tend to sway.[12]

But it is not enough to come to a halt with this prospect for communism's expansion among the backward nations. In terms of anticipating the trends of world history, what is even more important for us to realize is that individual eco-

[12] See also Sidney Hook, "Grim Report: Asia in Transition," *New York Times Magazine*, April 5, 1959.

nomic improvement, even at best, is not likely to come fast enough to satisfy the aspirations of the people. For in every underdeveloped nation, economic growth—with the exception of an increase in foodstuffs—is, at first, essentially a process of accumulating capital goods under forced draft, of alleviating as quickly as possible the crippling capital scarcity of the past. This necessarily means that the pace of *tangible* advance in the living standards of the masses is very slow, and nearly as imperceptible in communist nations with huge growth rates as in "mixed-economy" nations with smaller rates. Dams, reservoirs, roads, education, steel mills—all the basic necessities for advance—cannot be consumed, do not replace ragged clothes and hovels.

In this situation even the most sincerely motivated and efficient government is apt to find itself with an impatient and dissatisfied populace. Thus despite—or worse, because of—their all-out economic and social effort, fast-growing but still impoverished economies are likely to be impelled to seek incentives other than the self-sustaining impetus of economic improvement. These incentives may take the form of sheer compulsion, as has been the case in the communist states. But there is as well another means of mobilizing the stamina and morale needed to sustain the great ascent. This is the conscious direction of aspirations *away* from material ends, toward glory, conquest, or faith. In a word, it is the employment of a fierce and often bellicose nationalism as a compensation for the inevitable disappointments of the early stages of economic growth.

We have seen the development of such a nationalism in virtually every nation which has begun the steep economic climb. In China as well as in Russia there has been recourse not only to a deliberately stimulated patriotism, but to the encouragement of smoldering grudges against colonialism and capitalism. In dictatorships of a more rightist leaning, such as Egypt, nationalistic incentives and diversions of a still cruder nature have been used: the reawakening of ancient loyalties and racialisms, the fanning of atavistic military and religious ambitions, the appeal, as in the days of heroic history, to the memories of the past.

It is probable that a degree of inflamed nationalism is an inseparable concomitant of forced economic development. The unfortunate result is that an era which could be a prelude to building for a great future runs the grave risk of becoming instead a period of heightened tensions and increased chances for the destruction even of present frail standards. The spread of high aspirations to the peoples whose conditions are now the least human on earth is a great and irreversible drama of our times, but during our lifetimes the drama promises to be as tragic as it may ultimately be ennobling.

What is likely to be the full impact on America of this challenge of economic development is a matter to which we shall return in our next chapter. But at this point, while we are reflecting on the nature of the history which is closing in upon and constricting our traditional optimistic plans, it may be useful to take one last view of the problem. For it is certain that the transition ahead will be ugly, and that the latent susceptibility to unrest and to political and economic extremism within the developing countries will exert tremendous and disturbing pressures on ourselves. What we would do well to remember in our consequent concern and likely irritation is that for many generations these submerged populations of the world suffered the impact of a Western dynamism whose purposes they did not understand and whose disruptions they could not control. Now they return their blows upon the West just as incomprehensibly and with just as staggering force. This is indeed a time of great trial for the West. But we must bear in mind that what is a closing-in of history for us, is an opening-out of history for most of the peoples of the world.

7. *The Drift Away from Capitalism*

Heretofore we have been concerned with the historic consequences of two great currents of world development: that of science in general and the atomic weaponry in particular, and that of the spread of popular aspirations, as it manifests itself in the revolutionary upthrust of the underdeveloped world. Now we must turn to a third current of world change which, as we shall see, derives much of its internal momentum from the trends we have already discussed. This third current is a basic change in the economic orientation of the world—a change we have already noted in the backward nations but which we can now deal with in generalized terms as affecting the advanced nations no less. It can be described as the collectivization of twentieth-century economic life.

Once again, however, it is well for us to approach this current of history in the concrete guise by which it makes itself visible and meaningful to us. And this immediate guise can be very simply stated. It is this: over the larger part of our history, we have faced a future in which our own form of economic organization, capitalism, was the triumphant and dominant form of economic and social organization in the world. This is no longer true. Today and over the foreseeable future, traditional capitalism throughout most of the world has been thrown on a defensive from which it is doubtful that it can ever recover. As a capitalist nation we are no longer riding with the global tides of economic evolution, but against them.

This is a transformation of contemporary history which is at one and the same time an indisputable reality of the recent past and a bitterly contested prospect for the future. Of all the transformations affecting the lineaments of the future, it is the one toward which we feel the greatest resistance and the least willingness to set ourselves at an intellectual remove. The result is that a trend of history which should be the object of dispassionate study and understanding, and which is of the greatest moment for our survival, becomes either ignored or seriously misinterpreted.

Let us begin by very briefly documenting the history of the transformation itself.

The nineteenth and early twentieth centuries, as we know, were the era of capitalist growth. Within a century of its first full bloom in the Industrial Revolution, capitalism had reached out to become the commanding economic structure of the

Western world. Most of Europe, North America, Scandinavia, even the Antipodes, became market-oriented, profit-stimulated, industrially based economies. In all of them the acknowledged leadership of the social order was vested in the business world, whose purposes, values, and methods were broadly similar from one nation to the next. Meanwhile, as we have already seen, these countries in turn exerted their influence over a vast portion of the non-capitalist world—that is, over its unindustrialized areas. In the last thirty years of the nineteenth century alone, Britain, France, and Germany acquired domain over 125 million people and nine million square miles of territory.

By 1913 the conquest of capitalism appeared complete. It had either displaced, or was fast crowding out, the previous feudal economies. No other competitor of any degree of power even remotely appeared to challenge its pre-eminence. It is some testimony to the solidity of the capitalist system that until 1917 no major government in the world had ever been headed by a Labor Party, much less by a socialist regime of any description.

Yet this genuinely impressive accomplishment was now succeeded by a still more astonishing denouement. For the progressive success of capitalism over ten generations was to be undermined in less than two. In 1913 socialism was still the economic utopia of a dissident minority movement, without either the respectability of official government power, or the possession, however disreputable, of de facto power. Forty years later, in various guises, socialism as an economic reality had swept around the world. The Sino-Soviet enclave alone embraced a population twice as large as the whole capitalist world of 1913. Among the new nations emerging from the rapid break-up of the colonial portion of that world, virtually all bore the stamp of socialist orientation. More significant yet, within the erstwhile citadel of capitalism, nation after nation had defected from the ranks of orthodoxy. By 1959, in Australia, Belgium, Denmark, France, Germany, Iceland, Italy, Netherlands, New Zealand, Norway, Sweden, and the United Kingdom—all staunchly capitalist governments in 1913—a so-called "Socialist" administration had at least once come into power; and in most of these nations it was either still in power or now headed the party of the Opposition. That this was a very different kind of "socialism" from the communist organization of society in the East was, of course, apparent. And yet even more than the spread of militant communism and of anti-colonial revolutions, it was symptomatic of a basic and fundamental swing in the world's economic orientation. For it made apparent that *within* the capitalist powers themselves, the unquestioned supremacy of the old capitalist ideologies had been challenged by a new set of guiding ideas.

8. *The Historic Role of Communism*

How are we to account for this world-wide phenomenon?

It is clear, to begin with, that the trend away from capitalism is not a simple but a complex historic development. It is patently impossible to consider as part of a single movement the communist revolutions in Russia or China, and the emergence of socialist governments in postwar England or Scandinavia. But it may help us gain an understanding of the over-all economic redirection of our times if we start by picturing the communist and the Western European nations as the opposite ends of a spectrum of "socialist" economic organization. When we then compare the salient characteristics of the infra-red and the conservative blue ends of this spectrum, a very obvious but nonetheless important contrast strikes us. This is the difference in the stage of economic development of the two groups.

The Western nations, at the conservative end of the economic line-up, all have their developmental days behind them. This is not to say that their economic expansion is finished. But it builds atop an already firmly established foundation. The communist nations, on the other hand, are without exception in the process of industrialization. Some, like China, are barely out of the subsistence-agrarian level; others like Russia appear as half-finished skyscrapers whose enormous framework has not yet been made suitable for occupancy. But note that with the exception of Czechoslovakia, which was won by coup, and East Germany, which fell as a war prize, no nation has gone communist which was not then a peasant economy.

This contrast of stages of development now suggests an important point. It is that communism, as a major economic movement of today, is playing the same role as did capitalism in the seventeenth and eighteenth centuries. For the Western "socialist" nations have also gone through their periods of repression and severity in the course of their own transitions from agrarian to industrial societies. These periods were considerably milder than present-day communism because the transitions began at a higher level of well-being and because they were then the vanguard and not the rearguard of advance. But one who recoils at the rigors and suffering of the Chinese and Russian transformations would do well to compare these travails with those of the West in its early capitalist throes. He will then find striking—and perhaps discomfiting—similarities between the movement of the Western pre-industrial world into capitalism and that of the East into communism. Behind both lies the impulsion for material growth and the leverage of a newly unleashed industrial technique. In both systems large volumes of savings are brought into being, concentrated in a few hands, and redirected back into the further development of the industrial framework. More important in terms of social reorganization is the forcible transfer of masses of workers from farm to industry—a process which took place by the enclosure of the peasant's land under early capitalism and by the collectivization of his land under communism. Again, in both transitions we find the social agonies attendant upon the violent redirection of a traditional, earth-bound, static way of life into a future-oriented, organized, electric tempo of modern existence. And finally, under capitalist as well as communist industrialization the human cost has been very great. Every student of early capitalism is shocked at the inhumanity of its conditions of labor and at the heartlessness of its ruling classes. We see a similar grinding of the human personality in communism today.

We have already touched on the reasons why developing nations today are likely candidates for communism rather than capitalism. What we must now add to our understanding is that communism, in the present stage of world history, is not so much the successor to but the *substitute* for capitalism. It is the manner in which the backward nations seek to reproduce in a few decades the transformations which capitalism carried out over two centuries.

This perspective on communism serves to clarify more than its "functional" appeal. It also calls our attention away from the manifest revolutionary aspect of the communist movement to its concealed inertial core. Much of what we identify in communism as its most distinctive features—its cruelties, its use of terror, its indifference to personal liberties—is not so much the face of the new world as the shadow of the old. For the nations which are now being goaded and guided on their long march are not only economically backward; they are also without a history of gradual political elevation and social enlightenment. As a result, for all its claim to be part of the wave of the future, communism is often helplessly entangled in the undertow of the past.

Thus John Gunther reminds us that Russia has had only *one* moderately free election in its entire history (and this one just *after* the Bolshevik *coup d'état*). Gunther writes:

> Some remarkable precursors of things to come may be noted in the old Russia. Terror, as an instrument of punitive assault on an entire class, began with Ivan the Terrible. . . . The keynotes of Russian policy in the nineteenth century were, in the words of one historian, "orthodoxy, autocracy, nationalism": what better words could describe the Soviet Union today?[13]

In China we find the same historic background of iron rule, so "total" in character that one historian has singled it out as a form of government properly designated as "Oriental Despotism."[14] As Richard Hughes, an experienced British correspondent, comments: "Too much Western sympathy is wasted upon communism's destruction of personal liberties and aspirations in China. The Honorable Middle Kingdom has endured totalitarian methods for centuries. The Confucian mandarins were as tyrannical and absolutist in their administration under the Emperors as the cadres and Communist party members are today under Mao."[15]

Such considerations by no means exculpate the misdeeds of Russia and China. "[Communism's] unfortunate association with violence encourages a certain evil tendency in human beings," Nehru has written in a well-known statement.[16] No

[13] *Inside Russia Today* (New York, 1957), pp. 153-54, 164.
[14] Karl Wittfogel, *Oriental Despotism* (New Haven, Conn., 1957).
[15] *New York Times Magazine*, November 2, 1958.
[16] *New York Times Magazine*, September 7, 1958.

impartial history of the communist movement can slur over the fact that both in Russia and China there existed at least the seeds of a political and intellectual liberalism which communism brutally chopped off at the roots; and for this telling blow at the future, communism must bear the present responsibility, and must itself pay the ultimate price. Nor does the inertial— as opposed to the revolutionary—source of its momentum in any way lessen the threat of communism to the West. Indeed, culturally and intellectually, it reinforces it.

Nevertheless one must also view the other side of the coin. To retreat before the violence and cruelty of communism, without recognizing on the one hand the historic roots of that cruelty, and on the other, our failure to offer an alternative route of development as speedy and efficacious, is to vent a moral indignation which is shallow, or worse, arrogant. One need not condone excesses which are frequently sickening, or rhapsodize over an upheaval whose potential for world disturbance we have already seen. But it is only moral cowardice to single out the evils of communism, while refusing to admit to what may ultimately be the beneficial consequences of the tremendous economic movement which it is effecting. What will happen to the harsh disciplining forces of the communist system once the great transition has been made we do not know. But surely the hope of the future rests in the possibility that with communism, as with capitalism, the completion of the industrial transformation may soften and mellow the rigors of the transitional phase.

9. *The Historic Role of Western "Socialism"*

It is a very different aspect of the world's economic re-orientation which we encounter when we now turn to its manifestations in Western Europe. Unlike the violent changes we have been discussing in the communist or the underdeveloped nations, the changes in Europe are mild, slow, obscure. Indeed, the first question they raise is whether, despite the emergence of "socialist" governments and parties in almost all European nations, this is really a movement away from capitalism at all.

For certainly by the Marxian touchstone of economic identification—property ownership—what we find here is hardly a revolutionary change. Even under the most ambitious socialist programs, as for instance that of Great Britain after the war, the nationalization of industry has been limited to a few sick or strategic sectors, and has been accompanied by the most meticulous compensation of former owners. Meanwhile the market mechanism and the profit motive, those capitalist motors of progress, continue to provide the basic economic impetus. If a heavily predominant private ownership and a profit-making direction of business constitute the hallmarks of capitalism, then Europe is unquestionably still capitalist.

Yet, just as unquestionably, it is not the capitalism of old. For if Europe is not socialist by any of the traditional criteria, it is nonetheless characterized by a phenomenon commonly associated with socialism. This is the growth of public control over and intervention into private economic life—of *planning* as an integral part of the economic system. Whether we look to the British "managed economy" or the French *économie dirigée*, to the Swedish "middle way," or even to the German *soziale Marktwirtschaft*, this is the most noticeable change in the character of European capitalism. It is the metamorphosis of a system of *laissez faire* into one of mild national economic collectivism.

Hence we must begin to consider the Western aspect of the world's economic transformation by asking what is the cause and the meaning of this drift toward planning. For it should be clear that the implications of this change are in some respects more historically significant than the far bolder leap into communism. That leap cannot by any stretch of the imagination be called a natural and spontaneous outgrowth of its societies. In every case it has been a drastic and discontinuous change, imposed upon a passive peasantry by a small revolutionary faction. But this is not at all the case with the European metamorphosis. Here we see *capitalism itself* in the process of change. As part of the historic future, what is going on here is more portentous for the capitalist outlook than the radical by-passing of capitalism by the communist "short cut" into industrialization.

We need not retrace the long and complex history of Europe's economic centralization. Many forces contributed to its

103

growth, including not least the powerful economic demands of total war. Whereas as late as the Boer War the mounting of an armed offensive required no more than a fractional diversion of the normal output of the economy, beginning with World War I the demands of war threatened to burst the capacity of the "normal" economy. During the first great war, as Crane Brinton writes, "All countries . . . sooner or later felt obliged to introduce drastic economic planning, which anticipated in some sense the more collectivistic economy of today. Everywhere war appeared, as the American President Madison's dictum has it, as 'the mother of executive aggrandizement.' "[17]

But it was not alone the blows of war which pressed the European economy toward collectivism. More fundamental yet was a process which lay at the heart of the capitalist dynamic itself. This was the tendency of business enterprise to enlarge, ramify, agglomerate its scale of production.

From the beginning an expansive *élan* had been an outstanding attribute of capitalism. The growth of a pinpoint enterprise to an acre tract, the stretching of a small operation of manufacture into a complex assembly line—this technological virtuosity had always been one of the primary characteristics of the capitalist system. But it had also been—although it remained for Marx to point this out—the cause of a mounting social and economic *vulnerability* of the system.

For the consequences of this agglutination of productive power was to magnify many-fold the dangers inherent in that

---

[17] Crane Brinton and others, *A History of Civilization* (New York, 1957), vol. II, p. 448.

endemic weakness of capitalism, its recurrent economic recessions. From the third decade of the nineteenth century,
economists had begun to discern regular reversals of trade that
interrupted the normal course of economic expansion. But
these depressions, which might be shrugged off as useful
economic winnowing mechanisms when they eliminated only
small and isolated units of enterprise, could no longer be so
stoically accepted when the threatened victims were giant enterprises whose fall could imperil a whole industry, even a
whole economy.

The result, as E. H. Carr has described it, was that when
severe depression rocked the entire capitalist system in the
late 1920's and 1930's, "it was the capitalists—the industrialists,
farmers, and financiers—who . . . begged the state to save
them by laying the foundation of an ordered economy."

Professor Carr goes on to comment:

> They were fully justified in doing so. The structure
> of industry and finance in the twentieth century had
> been so firmly integrated and concentrated that its main
> sectors were no longer separable from one another or
> from the national economy as a whole. It was unthink-
> able that a great bank or a great railway, a major unit
> in the steel or chemical industries, should be wound up
> for failing to meet its obligations. Far from watching the
> economic struggle from the heights of Olympian aloof-
> ness, the state had to step into the ring to save the poten-
> tial loser from being knocked out. No doubt, the bank-
> ers and industrialists who in the hour of distress invoked
> state support did not fully realize the implications of
> their action. . . . But what had been done could not

be wholly undone. . . . The conception of a national economy had taken root; and by the same token some kind of planning authority had become inevitable . . .[18]

Thus the movement toward planning, far from being in its origins a radical evolution beyond capitalism, must be understood as constituting a protective device for capitalism. Government control and intervention have been the means by which, on the one hand, capitalism was able to co-ordinate its production for the efficient prosecution of war and, on the other hand, by which it sought to guard against its growing vulnerability to economic crisis.

And yet it is also perfectly clear that by no means all the European planning movement is merely such a protective device. Whereas war planning as such, or the rationalization of production under the fascist corporate state, or the attempts to mitigate the business cycle, or the emergence of pan-European "communities" of iron and steel and coal production can all be seen as essentially *conservative* planning efforts, it is apparent that much of European planning has a different purpose. It concerns itself with social welfare—not so much with the production as with the redistribution of wealth. We find elaborate planning mechanisms for the distribution of aid and allowances to the unemployed and the aged, for the provision of subsidies to multi-child families, for public services such as Britain's National Health Service. We find a limited but by no means dormant planning movement toward nationalization of industry. We encounter an insistence on full employment as an overriding goal of economic policy.

[18] *The New Society,* Beacon ed. (Boston, 1957), pp. 28-29.

These are aspects of planning which clearly fall outside the general description of planning as a conservative protective mechanism. Americans would tend to identify these uses of planning as evidences of "welfare capitalism." But our own identification of them directly emphasizes the critical element in the evolutionary picture of European capitalism. In Europe the historic movement toward reform and welfare has not been identified with a capitalist tag. On the contrary it has been universally identified with the political ideology of socialism.

10. *Europe at the Halfway Station*

We have already described the roots of socialism in the underdeveloped world. There, in large part, it is espoused as a "functional" means of rivaling the material works of capitalism. But the roots of socialism in Europe are of a different kind. More than anything else they reflect an inadequacy of long standing in the political workings of capitalism.

To be sure there was also an inadequacy of economic performance—low wage rates, highly unequal income distribution, recurrent unemployment—all of which have been powerful factors in the promotion of socialism. Yet beyond this was a deeper failure of the European capitalist system. It was an inability to include the ambitions and aspirations of its lower orders within its own ideological framework. From the beginning, capitalism in Europe has been a self-consciously bourgeois institution, frankly suspicious of, not to say hostile to, the aims of its laboring classes. Nothing of the social consensus which bound up the American class divisions ever characterized the European scene. In America, Horatio Alger may have been only a myth, but in Europe even the myth did not exist.

Thus the direction in which working class ambitions and aspirations naturally gravitated was toward the quarter of socialism. No capitalist power in Europe ever thought to rally its working classes with the slogans of the bourgeoisie. It is a revealing fact that in their moments of greatest reliance on popular support—in the conduct of war—their governments relied not on economic but on patriotic motives. The soldiers of France fought for *la patrie* not for *le capitalisme*. The Germans who responded to the call of *das Vaterland* would scarcely have been expected to troop to the colors for *Der Kapitalismus*. In contrast, the idea of socialism has traditionally provided a European mass rallying cry. Russian soldiers fought for their *socialist* Fatherland against German soldiers who fought as willingly for their National *Socialism*.

As the example makes very clear, the realities behind the idea of socialism were often vague and contradictory. Nevertheless, in the word was a symbol of something which capitalism never achieved in its own name: a drive for social justice, an often crudely formulated but passionately felt movement toward the dismantling of economic privilege, and an ideological concern for the needs of the least favored and most numerous members of society. To the European lower classes

—and to their powerful representatives among the intellectuals —socialism was a movement freighted with great destinies for the future, while capitalism was a system weighted with the irreparable injustices of the past. It was this ideological orientation, combined with the mechanisms of planning—neutral or even conservative in themselves—which provided the anti-capitalist momentum of European economic evolution.

To some extent this identification of reform as "socialist" persists in Europe today. As Professor Carr has written:

> You cannot in these days plan for inequality. Once you can no longer explain inequalities either as the salutary result of a natural economic process or as incidentals in an economic organization primarily designed to prepare for war, it must become a main purpose of economic policy to eliminate them. This is the political connection between planning and socialism. In theory they are separable; historically they spring from different sources. But, once the historical evolution of the capitalist system has made a controlled and planned economy necessary, and once the temporary expedient of planning for war has become obsolete, to plan for socialism is the only available alternative.[19]

There are signs, however, that the socialist inspiration for reform is today somewhat on the wane. In most European countries the aims and purposes of the socialist parties are confused and unsure. The frightening totalitarianism of Russia, the disappointments of nationalization in Great Britain have taken much of the wind out of socialist sails. The political problem of democratic rule, which in the past socialism

[19] *Op. cit.*, p. 39.

always shrugged off as secondary to the economic problem of control, has now reasserted itself with terrible emphasis. And the revelation that nationalization is no cure for the grinding realities, the dull tasks, the necessary hierarchies of the industrial process has made it clear that if socialism is to offer nothing more than nationalization it is scarcely to be preferred to a well-managed capitalism.

Hence the socialist movement in Europe is conservative. Unlike communism in the backward countries it has no overriding goal of economic development for a starving people with which to "justify" the means it uses. For the moment it contents itself with pressing in the direction of "welfare"—toward greater income equality, the extension of social services, and the diminution of social privilege. None of this is in any sense "revolutionary." More important yet, the sponsorship of reform is more and more ceasing to be the exclusive property of the Left, with the result that even the intellectual core of the socialist movement has increasing difficulty in defining how its program differs from that of at least the more enlightened conservative parties.[20]

But it is much too early to say that the socialist movement in Europe has spent its force. Its waning in recent years has corresponded with a period of unprecedented boom; given a serious recession, a further series of defeats and humiliations along the lines of the Algerian fiasco, a move toward power by the lingering reactionary elements, and a reactivation of the socialist ideological drive is by no means unlikely. Totally unlike the situation in America, capitalism in Europe is *on trial*. There

[20] Cf. *New Fabian Essays* (London, 1952).

is no guarantee, however, that should it fail it would be replaced by the socialism of an earlier vintage. As Hitler's National Socialism has unforgettably shown, the forces of the extreme Right may also wear the brassards of the Left. Whether amid the strains of its global readjustment in power and prestige Europe will find an authoritarianism of the Right preferable to the slow evolution of its "bourgeois socialism" is unpredictable. In view of the rise of de Gaulle in France and the lurking evidences of reactionary nationalism in Germany, such a possibility is clearly not to be summarily ruled out.

In sum, it would seem that the Western European nations are at halfway stations along an historic road. If they are no longer identifiable as the capitalisms of twenty years ago, neither have they attained an organization of society which would correspond to the socialist aspirations of twenty years ago. Instead we find the "socialist" mechanisms of planning being used to buttress an essentially capitalist social and economic structure; and given a reasonable accommodation of erstwhile socialist aims, as in England, there is no reason why this halfway station should not endure for a considerable period.

Whatever may be its fate as an ideology, however, one aspect of socialism has become irreversibly fixed into place. This is the emergence of collective social and economic goals—for the most part of national scope, but to a growing extent of pan-European coverage—as an integral part of the European economic order. A subservience of individual enterprise to the state, very different from the pre-war *laissez faire*, has become a salient reality of economic life and an unquestioned axiom of economic philosophy. The political coloration of this mild

111

collectivism remains to be seen, as does the degree to which it may be "hardened" by the pressure of events. What is certain is that the historic road away from the unplanned capitalism of the past will not again be traversed in the opposite direction.

11. *The American Inquietude*

Against this last sweep of history the United States stands in a peculiarly exposed position. Virtually alone among the great powers of the world we still profess an unequivocal rejection of "socialist" ideals. Thus what we half see, half divine, as the meaning of the European economic movement fills us with unease. It seems to us incomprehensible that at the very time when capitalism, as we know it, has demonstrated its greatest economic and social success it should be thrown on the defensive and forced to adopt an "alien" collectivism in order to survive.

In our next chapter we shall take up the study of American capitalism in this regard. But before we leave our consideration of the world movement away from capitalism, it might be useful to reflect on two analogies which may serve to give some perspective to our present historic situation.

The first concerns the obvious fact that behind the ideological differences of European "socialism" and American "capitalism" there is an important convergence of realities. Most of the institutional welfare arrangements which bear the social-ist label abroad can be duplicated here under the label of capitalism. Many of the goals of social equality which the European socialists seek we already evidence. Yet between the *ideals* of "socialism" abroad and "capitalism" at home there is a deep mutual distrust and antipathy.

This contrast between a similarity of institutions and a clash of ideals recalls a similar situation of the late eighteenth and early nineteenth centuries. Then, it will be remembered, the subversive threat to America was thought to come from those nations whose principles of monarchy and aristocracy were deemed "irreconcilable" with those of democracy. Yet today we find democracy nowhere so firmly established as in the "monarchies" of England, Netherlands, Norway, Sweden, and Denmark. We must be careful that an aversion to the idea of socialism does not blind us to a similar identity of values and institutions between ourselves and the European "socialist" nations.

The second reflection concerns our failure to understand socialism as a movement of profound spiritual as well as ma-terial protest against the conditions of human life. Our maga-zines and newspapers, public speeches and books are quick to point up the inevitable failings of socialism, and never weary of calling to our attention the cruelties and repressions of com-munism. But such denunciations, far from arming us against or clarifying our understanding of socialism and communism, only serve to muddy our minds. They obscure the fact that the literature of socialist protest is one of the most moving and morally searching of all chronicles of human hope and despair. To dismiss that literature unread, to vilify it without the faintest conception of what it represents, is not only shocking but dangerously stupid.

It is well to recall here another analogy. It is frequently said that by its aggressions and cruelties communism has unredeemably tarnished the ideals which it may once have represented; and that by its pedestrian realities democratic socialism has effectively ended the Utopian vision from which it originally sprang. But such dismissals of the durability of socialist and communist ideologies are much too glibly made. They ignore the fact that for generations—indeed for centuries—millions of Europeans were willing to believe in the ideas and ideals of another great movement, despite its worldly shortcomings. It is very doubtful if the Church, in the days of its massacres of heretics, its Inquisitorial procedures, or its cynical leadership, would come off much better than communism from the point of view of a betrayal of original ideas. Yet throughout those years the Church endured because millions believed more strongly in the reality of its ideals than in the reality of the acts which defiled them.

It is clear that some such condition exists today in socialism and communism. Certainly history should teach us that it is only by penetrating to the inspirational fervor which they evoke, rather than by dwelling on their failures or glorying in their shame, that we can begin to understand the full force behind these secular religions of our time.

III

→→→ ←←←

THE
AMERICAN
COUNTER-
CHALLENGE

We have thus far been concerned with tracing some of the main currents of history in our times—the accelerating sweep of science and technology; the revolutionary extension of popular aspirations to the impoverished base of the human community; the economic reorientation, abrupt in some nations, gradual in others, away from the institutions and ideology of traditional capitalism. Yet our discussion up to this point has been only a partial consideration of the forces shaping our future. It has, so to speak, concerned itself mainly with the nature of the history which will come to us. What we have still to consider is the trajectory of our own momentum into the future—the American counterchallenge to the transformations which are so radically and rapidly altering the historic environment.

To find such a counterchallenge is not difficult. No matter from what angle of approach one examines American society, sooner or later one penetrates to a central driving force. This is our enormous economic momentum. There can be no doubt that our economic growth is the most powerful, the most all-pervasive, and the most important engine of our historic motion into the future.

It is not only because our economic momentum is so immediately visible that it commands our attention. It is also because our economic drive is our *chosen* counterthrust to history. Unlike so many world developments, it is not a process which we are seeking to shore up, to decelerate, to deflect. On the contrary, in our economic progress we find an instance in which the history we seek to make accords with that which impersonal forces are also bringing about. We tend to see in our growth a vehicle of an optimistic destiny—a force admittedly immense and even at times shaking, but essentially propitious and benign.

What we do not consider, however, when we contemplate this promising vista, is that our economic momentum does not come to an end in the simple increase of physical wealth. In the process of economic expansion there are unnoticed consequences, and in the achievement of greater abundance there are concealed implications which offer a more sobering prospect than those we commonly hold. And finally in the bland trust in economic growth itself as an effective counterchallenge to the closing-in of history may very well lie the most crucial of all those beliefs which the assaults of an unfriendly age is forcing America to reconsider.

1. Looking Backward

This chapter will concern itself with economic growth as the main avenue down which we proceed to our historic future. Therefore, it is well for us to begin by reviewing a development whose general outlines are well known, but whose implications continue to be of fresh interest. This is the extraordinary increase in living standards which our growth has produced over the past thirty years.

In the economic folklore of our country we still look back to 1929 not only as a year of great business prosperity but as a year of widespread and fundamental well-being. But when we examine the economy of 1929 critically, we find that the façade of business prosperity concealed an inner structure of widespread economic frailty.

In *The Big Change*, Frederick Lewis Allen described the situation succinctly:

> During that very year 1929, according to the subsequent estimates of the very careful and conservative Brookings Institution, only 2.3 percent of American families had incomes of over $10,000 a year. Only 8 percent had incomes of over $5,000. No less than 71 per-

119

cent had incomes of less than $2,500. Some 60 percent had incomes of less than $2,000. More than 42 percent had incomes of less than $1,500. And more than 21 percent had incomes of less than $1,000 a year.

"At 1929 prices," said the Brookings economists, "a family income of $2,000 may be regarded as sufficient to supply only basic necessities." One might reasonably interpret this statement to mean that any income below that level represented poverty. *Practically 60 percent of American families were below it—in the golden year 1929!*[1]

Thus, in the year of America's optimal economic functioning up to that date, a condition of chronic insufficiency affected most of its working-class population. If $2,000 was the waterline of adequacy, then the stokers and firemen and humble sailors of the capitalist ship lived far below that line. In 1929 the National Industrial Conference Board found that wages in its twenty-three main industries averaged fifty-six cents an hour. Even with a 45-to-50-hour work week, such a wage yielded the average worker an income which fell short by a third of the Brookings minimum income for basic needs.

Whether or not this was the "fault" of capitalism is a matter to which we shall shortly return. But certainly we cannot properly appraise the justice of the share going to the bottom of the income pyramid without casting an eye on its golden apex. Of the $83 billion of total disposable income received in 1929—after federal income taxes and capital gains and losses—almost 19 per cent accrued to the top one per cent of income receivers. That is, some $15½ billion was divided among the one in every hundred households which were sit-

[1] *The Big Change* (New York, 1952), p. 144.

uated at the summit of the economic pyramid. Had one-half of this amount been divided instead among the nation's non-agricultural labor forces, the typical worker would have received an increase in pay of some $250. This would have meant a rise in his wage—which averaged $1,400—of almost a fifth.

Thus two facts characterized the economy in 1929. One was the clear connection of a general condition of insufficiency with the central income responsibility of capitalism—its wage payments. The other was the considerable *potential* alleviation of that insufficiency by a massive redistribution of income.

Yet underlying these facts was the intransigent reality that in 1929 *no* system of distribution would have yielded entirely satisfactory results. For the overriding actuality of that age of great "prosperity" was an economic inability to produce enough to provide a good standard of living for all. In 1929 had the nation's disposable income been divided equally among all thirty-six million households, the result would have been an income of $2,300 per household—about halfway between a living standard of bare necessities and one of minimal comfort. No doubt for the two-thirds of the population whose standard was below this such an egalitarian division of the nation's output would have brought very great benefits. But we must also face up squarely to the fact that an income ceiling of $2,300 would have imposed upon society—and especially on its creative elements—a stifling sense of economic scarcity. Egalitarianism, pushed to its extreme, would have meant an inconceivable social transformation, not alone politically but in the quality of the existence it would have imposed on the nation as a whole.

2. The Upward Shift

When we now turn to the economic profile of the nation three decades later, a striking change meets our eye. Something like a huge social escalation process, a massive migration upward through the income strata, has taken place.

In the table below we can see this change, after adjusting 1929 figures to 1958 values:

INCOME DISTRIBUTION IN 1929 AND 1958[2]

Income levels, 1958	Per cent of all households with equivalent of this income in 1929	Per cent of all households with this actual income in 1958
less than $2,000	21	14
$2,000–$ 3,000	21	10
$3,000–$ 4,000	18	12
$4,000–$ 5,000	11	13
$5,000–$10,000	21	38
over $10,000	8	13

[2] *Survey of Current Business*, April, 1959, p. 14; 1929 figures from Brookings figures previously quoted, adjusted upward for reasons of statistical comparability by 100 per cent. This is considerably more than the 70-80 per cent price change and therefore conservatively understates the escalation which has taken place. The figures for 1958 are broken at the $3,000 and $5,000 levels at the same frequency distributions as obtain in the finer income distribution analysis for 1957.

What we see in this tabular panorama is clearly not just a static comparison. It is a pair of balance sheets which testifies to a dynamic social interim—a wholesale vertical shift of living standards. If we take $4,000 as an approximate 1958 equivalent of the Brookings minimum level of adequacy, we see that whereas only 40 per cent of all households in America had passed this mark in 1929, by 1958 some 64 per cent of all households were above it.[3]

But the 1958 panorama of incomes can be given yet a further social significance. It is that most of the remaining stratum of substandard incomes—a group which still comprised a third of the nation's households—was attributable to *social* rather than economic malfunctioning. In large part it was traceable to the racial injustice which pushed the average level of non-white incomes 50 per cent below the level for whites. In part it was due to the isolation of backwash agricultural communities. In part it reflected the destitution of old age, and of physical and mental handicap. These kinds of poverty were no less real for being "social" in origin, and indeed may have been even more intractable for that reason. Nevertheless, national poverty in 1958 presented a meaningful contrast to 1929. In that earlier year, as we have seen, the major part of economic misfortune was rooted in the inadequate *productivity* of the industrial process itself. In 1958 this most obdurate of all barriers had been largely overcome. And this essentially technological fact was possessed of an important social consequence. It meant that the wage payments of capitalism no longer reflected an underlying economic limitation for which

[3] *Op. cit.*, p. 11, table 2.

capitalism, as a social system, could not be held responsible. In a few notoriously low-paid industries such as hotels or laundries or tobacco, wages were still below the waterline of adequacy. But with the rising productivity of the main body of the system this was no longer a general condition. When the average worker in the nation earned $4,324, there was no doubt that the wage structure of capitalism as a whole had severed the connection between poverty and industrial earnings.

Equally significant was another radical change since 1929—the sharp decline in the potential benefits of income redistribution. For the rise from the bottom had also been accompanied by a fall from the top—in fact by a fall which was very possibly the most severe shrinkage of income shares ever to affect any dominant class in history short of revolution. In 1929, as we have seen, the upper one per cent enjoyed nearly 19 per cent of the nation's disposable income. By 1958 that share had shrunk by over half to less than 9 per cent.[4] Undoubtedly these statistics somewhat overstate the decline, since they do not reflect the greatly increased use of expense accounts as a privileged means of smuggling income, or the money flows received as capital gains and then masked with paper losses, or certain non-taxable (and hence legally non-reported) income. But such caveats at best blur rather than erase the change.

For unquestionably the potential for income redistribution has been greatly diluted in the past 30 years. If we make the same hypothetical redistribution of half the income of the top one per cent in 1958, we find that the wages of the work

---

[4] *Statistical Abstract*, 1956, p. 304, table 364; also *Survey, op. cit.*, p. 14, table 5. The latest figure shown in the latter source is for 1957 when the top ranking 1.2 per cent of all families and individuals got 9.1 per cent of all income after taxes.

force, instead of being increased by nearly a fifth, as in 1929, would have risen by less than a fifteenth.

This is not to argue against further egalitarian measures. The leveling which characterizes the whole is certainly not true in the individual instance, where one man's income may still exceed another's by a thousandfold or more. Nor is it to claim that diminishing disparities of income levels by themselves provide a fully adequate description of American economic life. We must place against the undoubted narrowing of income differences the persistence of enormous inequalities of property in the economic structure. Despite sweeping claims of the democratization of ownership associated with "People's Capitalism," there is very little, if any, evidence of a significant widening of the concentrated ownership and control of the American corporate structure.[5] A staff report of the Senate Committee on Banking and Currency, in 1955, pointed out that "less than one per cent of all American families owned over four-fifths of all publicly held stocks owned by individuals." Or again, a parade in *Fortune* magazine of the wealthiest men in the United States unearthed the hitherto little-known figure of Mr. Paul Getty, whose personal fortune, estimated at $700,000,000 was the equivalent of the personal assets of some 200,000 middle-income fellow citizens, or of some 350,000 households in the lower income brackets.

This persisting extreme concentration of property suggests the degree to which capitalism must be considered a system of tightly held privileges and power, as well as one of diffused responsibility and reward. It will remind us that when we

[5] Cf. V. Perlo, " 'People's Capitalism' and Stock Ownership," *American Economic Review*, June, 1958, esp. p. 341.

speak of the adaptation of "capitalism" to the challenges of our times we are dealing with the vested interests of a small and immensely important group, as well as with the fragmented interests of the public at large.

But the persistence of property inequality does not alter the conclusion that there has been a deep and pervasive alteration in the palpable texture of American economic life. This has not, of course, taken place just in the thirty-year span to which we have directed attention. While the change in income *distribution* has been a significant new development, the rise in the level of mass well-being is only the culmination of a long history of economic growth. What makes the rise of the last thirty years of unique importance, however, is something more than the quantitative changes which have taken place. It is the difference in the *quality* of social existence which those changed quantities of income make possible. We have already seen that a total equalization of income in 1929 would have meant the social proletarianization of American society. In 1958 a similar hypothetical leveling would have brought a different outcome. The enormously larger disposable income of that year, divided equally among the 54 million household units of the nation, would have yielded an average income of just over $5,600. This would have enforced a very considerable compression of living standards for the upper half of the nation. But it no longer suggests a crushing deformation of American life. An egalitarian standard in 1958 would have meant no worse than a uniform lower-middle-class standard of existence.

3. The Prospect Ahead

It is when we consider this *qualitative* aspect of our quantitative growth that the future significance of America's economic momentum becomes apparent. Even by 1980 a continuance of the growth pattern of the last three decades will have made a noticeable difference in the quality of our social environment. Twenty years hence, if our momentum is sustained, the level of average family income will have risen to at least $8,000, allowing for a population rise to 235 million, and calculating in terms of today's prices. Some estimates place the prospective average family income of 1980 at $10,000 or higher. But what we must realize is that even the conservative figure of $8,000 is well above the median income of all professional and semi-professional, managerial and self-employed personnel for 1957—the most recent year for which we have such broad occupational statistics.[6] Thus our potential economic achievement over the next twenty years must be seen as the upgrading of an entire society to the point where its representative family enjoys a standard of living comparable to that of the upper middle class today. Such a condition of mass economic independence has never before characterized any large society.

[6] *Statistical Abstract*, 1959, p. 323, table 420.

To be sure we must beware of rosy oversimplifications. Growth will not automatically eliminate many of the existing pockets of poverty in America. As we have seen, much of this poverty is no longer connected functionally with the operation of the economy, and therefore does not directly share in its improvement. No realistic projection of national well-being twenty or even forty years hence can shrug off the likelihood that penury will continue to weigh upon underprivileged groups in society, unless we take deliberate measures to reintegrate them into the mainstream of activity.

But even with such a qualification—which, let us remember, today affects the life chances of at least one household in ten—it is without question an unprecedented economic prospect which lies before us. For if the economic momentum of our society will continue to manifest itself, there is no reason to stop at 1980. We must then look to our grandchildren's time, another twenty years ahead. And now the prospect becomes genuinely startling in its implications. Given a maintenance of the trend of growth, we can confidently expect an ordinary factory worker in that day to earn an income equal to at least $10,000. Looking yet another generation ahead, the Twentieth Century Fund estimates that a working American a century hence will produce as much in a seven-hour day as he now does in a forty-hour week. This quintupling of productivity would mean in effect that a factory worker could earn the equivalent of $15,000 to $20,000 while working only four days a week.

Such projections, as we shall see, may well never be attained. But even as mere "projections" they reveal the essential factor about the American economic drive. This is its socially revolutionary quality. The drive into abundance is an historic force which, if fully realized, bids fair to change the nature of social organization as radically, and very likely as disconcertingly, as the equally revolutionary ascent from the static agricultural world to that of the industrial process. There is no doubt but that an environment of great abundance would represent the achievement of an age-old dream of mankind. But, as we shall see, it is also a prospect which raises as many questions and which poses as many difficulties for the survival of our society, *as it is presently constituted,* as did the immense prospects of the seventeenth and eighteenth centuries for the societies in which those dreams also became realities.

4. *The Prevalence of Optimism*

Heretofore we have talked about the historic movement of the American economy in descriptive terms, tracing its growth largely in terms of the rise in the living standards of its lower and middle classes. Now we must turn from description to analysis. For if lower and middle shares have steadily increased over the last thirty years, this has been primarily because there has been more to be shared. The growth which has made itself felt as an improvement in well-being has come about largely through a spectacular rise in total output. Hence behind the projection of a distant Society of Wealth, or a nearer society of upper-middle-class status, lies the basic assumption of a continuing dynamic of capitalist expansion. And so the first question we must explore is whether this assumption is a plausible one. What are the prospects for a continuing over-all growth of American capitalism?

Nothing is more astonishing than to contrast the general outlook on this question today with that of only twenty years ago. Then the central concern of economists was whether capitalism had not already come to the end of its historic era of rapid expansion, and was not perforce turning to a new stage of "mature"—i.e., static or more slowly expanding—existence. Not growth but stagnation was the premise from which most economic prognostication began.

Today an extraordinary change of thinking marks economic thought. The idea of stagnation is one which rarely if ever makes its appearance in the technical journals; the fear of a prospective exhaustion of the capitalist dynamic is confined to a fringe of dissenting opinion. There is no better indication of the general line of thought about the prospects for growth than the results of a symposium conducted by the Committee for Economic Development, a highly regarded business research organization. In 1957 the C.E.D. asked fifty economic authorities, not all of whom were American, what each considered "the most important economic problem to be faced by the United States in the next twenty years." The answers covered a wide variety of topics, from international relations to urban decay. Many papers concerned themselves with the inflationary consequences of growth, and a lesser

130

number with the uses or misuses to which growth might be put. *But not a single paper raised as its central problem the possible failure of the economy to grow.*[7]

This is certainly a reassuring change of views. But it is also a sufficiently important one to warrant asking on what the prevalence of optimism is founded.

In part it clearly rests on a rewakened *awareness* of the process of growth itself. The spectacle of the newer nations of the world caught up in the problems and frustrations of initial development has aroused in us a belated appreciation, both of the momentum of our own developmental history and of capitalism as a growth-producing system. Thus when the C.E.D. itself surveys the course of American economic history, it concludes that growth has proceeded primarily because of the *kind of society* we were, and that therefore, "unless the society changes in some radical fashion, the trend of growth can reasonably be expected to go on. For the main forces responsible for the past growth are still operating."[8]

But it is not only a resuscitated faith in the past which is responsible for the optimistic consensus today. There is also a vast sense of reassurance stemming from the extraordinary performance of the American economy since the war. Gloomy forecasts to the contrary, the economy did not collapse with the end of World War II, but instead displayed one of the most remarkable surges of expansion we have ever witnessed. This has led economists—in a mood of considerable chastisement—to search for the factors which had somehow been

[7] C.E.D., *Problems of United States Economic Development* (New York, 1958), vol. I.
[8] C.E.D., *Economic Growth in the United States* (February, 1958), p. 41.

"overlooked," and which could be expected to provide an expansionary impetus for the future.

These have not been difficult to find. One is the huge increase in the systematic search for new products and processes by which growth is constantly restimulated. Over the last ten years expenditures on organized research and development have grown from $2.6 to $13 billion, and the trend is still sharply upward. A second obvious factor is the rise in birth rates—the baby boom which promises us, by 1975, a population some 30 per cent larger than today. A third is the huge investment potential which is promised by automation and by the approaching conquest of space, not to mention the bright prospects of many smaller industries, such as plastics, air transport, etc. Yet another reason for the sanguine outlook is a widespread managerial awareness of the need for national economic expansion, and the long-range planning which increasingly guides the policy decisions of our main business firms. And not least is the knowledge that no democratic government can long remain in office if it permits a depression "to run its course."

5. Second Thoughts

This is a fairly impressive body of evidence and testimony. And yet the question must be asked if it is impressive enough. For amid the general celebration of the prospects for continued growth, something very much akin to the faith of the early Classical economists in the "inevitability" of progress has come to pervade the atmosphere. There has been a change from the skeptical—no doubt too skeptical—attitude of the late thirties and mid-forties to an attitude which now seems reluctant to probe for anything which might throw a damper on the prevailing enthusiasm.

Thus we find, for example, that a central aspect of our growth experience of the past two decades is one which few spokesmen for the future candidly discuss. This is the fact that our great boom did not begin until the onset of World War II, and that its continuance since then has consistently been tied to a military rather than to a purely civilian economic demand.

This chapter of economic history scarcely needs elaborate documentation. We endured the year 1939 with nine and a half million unemployed men and women—one person in every six out of the working force. Over the previous ten years our net per-capita growth had been zero, and as a matter of fact in 1939 we had not yet quite regained the peak of 1929 output. Thereafter, under the impact of war expenditure our economy grew with fabulous speed. From 1940 to 1945 output rose by over 50 per cent in real terms. There ensued the momentary crisis of reconversion to be followed by the even more impressive "peacetime" boom of 1945 to the present. But this boom was emphatically not a return to prewar conditions of normal growth. The economy had indeed been radically changed. In the first place, it emerged from the war years with the largest reserve of liquid purchasing power ever accumulated in our history. Personal savings, which had averaged only three or four billion dollars a year prior to the war climbed to $28 billion in 1945. In all, the war years gave us a total of $150 billion of deferred buying power which then flowed from open sluice gates to impart a tremendous stimulus to industry.

At the same time, the contribution of the military budget did not permanently decline. Following the war our major national security expenditures fell abruptly—although still averaging $17 billion in the low period 1947 to 1950. But with the advent of Korea they again climbed to $44 billion a year, or half their World War II peak. In all, from 1947 to 1957, our major security expenditures (which does not include veterans' payments) totaled over $325 billion, or more than the total of all private expenditures for plant and equipment—a sizable fraction of which was also undertaken in direct response to defense needs.

Hence it is impossible to credit the economic performance of the last twenty years just to the "forces" which were operative within capitalism in the past. Furthermore, a review of those forces is in itself none too reassuring an augury of steady expansion in the future. Many of the factors which can be cited today as promising our continued growth can also be discovered in the not too happy past. In 1920 we also enjoyed a birth rate which, while declining, was as high as that of the post-World War II baby boom: in fact between 1920 and 1930 our population grew from 106 million to 123 million—a rate quite comparable to that we foresee today. In addition the "growth industries" of today can be impressively matched with the propitious outlook for the growth industries of the twenties: aircraft, household appliances, chemicals, aluminum, motion pictures, radio, to mention but a few. Meanwhile during the decade of the twenties motor vehicle output rose by 300 per cent and gasoline consumption by 400 per cent—a harbinger of what was then the coming Age of Mass Transport. And so far as our current managerial outlook can be said to provide an assurance of an expanding economy, we must not forget a similar attitude of mind in the pre-Depression Age. Indeed it is fair to say that in the 1920's a degree of optimism never attained again marked the general business tone.

There are, to be sure, very important elements in our contemporary picture which were not present in the 1920's—the most important, of course, being the new role of the government. But the similarity between the *private* sectors, then and now, is enough to make one hesitant to base our economic prospects for the future solely on the "main forces" operating within capitalism, unless one is very sure that these main forces will not again lead, as in the twenties, through boom to bust.

6.   Solutions and Further Problems

Thus behind the general optimism that surrounds our out-look there is concealed a troublesome question: what would happen to our growth prospects in the absence of a core of military outlays?

For the moment such a question is only academic. Given the state of tension between ourselves and the Soviets and the technological nature of modern war, it is a strong likelihood that our core of military expenditures will grow. Indeed, as we have seen, our defense purchases, which now absorb about a tenth of our total national output, may very well take a seventh within the next decade.[9]

In other words, we may be faced, at least for the more immediate future, with a military wedge which is not only growing larger in absolute but in proportional terms. The economic consequences of such a penetration can be predicted with a great deal more clarity than its social effects. An expanding military sector would aid our growth, not only by the direct

[9] Cf. C.E.D., *Problems of United States Economic Development*, I, 29; and also *The Challenge to America: Economic and Social Aspects*, Rockefeller Bros. Fund (New York, 1958), p. 67.

economic activity it called into being, but also by the indirect stimulus it exerted on the rest of the economy. Insofar as our prevailing optimism is posited, tacitly or explicitly, on a rising base of defense outlays, it is well justified in taking growth for granted.

Yet this "solution" to the problem forces us to confront two unpleasant alternatives. The first is the prospect of an indefinite expansion of military spending—of a continuation of the present trend beyond the "one-seventh" fraction which is now the target for military growth. Such a slowly entering wedge of military expenditures would undoubtedly insure a continuous increase in the size of total output. But this statistically successful solution to the problem of growth would, of course, carry a steep social price. In the first place it would patently be more and more difficult to equate the rise in over-all production of such an economy with a corresponding increase in consumer well-being. And secondly, the continuing introduction of a wedge of non-consumable goods would soon set up uncontainable inflationary pressures on the civilian body of the economy. Short of a drastic tax program or direct controls of various sorts, it is doubtful that the militarization of the economy could progress very far without very serious price rises in every sector.

No one, however, wants or expects such a military "solution" to the growth problem, not alone because of its economic difficulties but on account of its social implications. Hence the fact that our growth may be underwritten for a number of years ahead by an expanding military subeconomy is generally assumed to be an interim condition. Sooner or later, it is believed, the military budget will stabilize. A new level of military capabilities will have been achieved, and thereafter, although it may have to be maintained and renewed, it will not continue to expand.

This may very well be the case. But once this stage of military stability is reached, we must face the second alternative. This is a return to a reliance on the private forces of growth. For after the military wedge ceases to force its way into the economic system, the continued expansion of that system again devolves upon the impetus of the "main forces" of private investment. Hence we return to the question: What if those forces should fail?

The question is not meant to raise the specter of a depression of the duration and social anguish of the 1930's. The causes for the *extent and severity* of the Great Depression—the flimsiness of our banking and corporate structures, the suicidal selfishness of our foreign economic policy, the tragic misconception of the role of our government in combating an economic reversal —these fearful elements of our 1930's ordeal have largely been removed. But the *instability* which produced the Great Depression and, before it, a whole history of cyclical depressions, is another thing. There is no sign that this endemic weakness of capitalist growth has been removed. On the contrary there is every evidence that our growth is still subject to severe and possibly protracted intermissions. We have already suffered a "traditional" setback in the recession of 1957-58, when expenditures for plant and equipment in the manufacturing sector fell from $16 billion to about $11.5 billion. This was the principal reason for the rise of unemployment to over five million. And yet we were fortunate. Had the construction industry also declined, as has been the frequent case in past recessions, the impact of the 1957–58 recession could have been much more severe. Unemployment might then have risen above seven million and we would have faced an initial economic shock at least as severe as that of 1929.

And there are other signs of weakness in addition to our continuing susceptibility to investment instability. For a whole year *before* the downturn in mid-1957, our growth in per-capita living standards had been nil: our "growing" economy was doing no more than keeping abreast of a growing population, rather than forging ahead of it. In other words our rate of "normal" investment was by no means enough to advance our actual conditions of life. Meanwhile, the recession itself has highlighted still another historic source of economic vulnerability. This is the threat of technological unemployment, now magnified by the alarming technical possibilities of automation. In early 1959 industrial production had regained its 1957 level—but it was turning out the same flow of goods with some 750,000 fewer employees.

These instances from the recent past make it plain that, in and of themselves, the "main forces" of private expansion cannot guarantee a strong and steady rate of growth—even during a period of heavy military expenditure. This is a fact which even the staunchest believers in the vitality of private enterprise would admit. But, they would argue, this does not mean that the economy must therefore stagnate or decline. It is possible for government expenditure to step into the breach —if need be through deficit financing. Growth can be maintained, even if at a somewhat slower pace, by using the tools of anti-recession policy.

Undoubtedly this is true. But what the facile answer of

"compensatory government spending" does not always take into consideration is the *magnitude* of spending that may be involved. For as our economy grows, the absolute size of the annual investments needed to *keep* it growing also rises. Today, with a $450 billion economy, we must make yearly additions of some $30 billion to plant and equipment to keep moving ahead at our modest pace. By 1980, if our economy has grown at the rate anticipated by most optimistic predictors, our total output will be in the range of $900 billion. By then our required annual addition to plant and equipment will be $50 to $60 billion, in today's values. Now let us imagine a drop of some 30 per cent in this expenditure, as was the case in 1957, and we see that the amount of necessary compensatory spending, if our rate of growth is to be maintained, would be an extra $15 to $20 billion a year, over and above the normal government budget. Imagine further the by no means improbable coincidence that construction activity fell simultaneously with plant and equipment expenditures. In such an eventuality the necessary government injections to maintain our momentum unchecked could rise to $30 to $40 billion—a year. Finally, if we reserve the possibility even if not the likelihood, of a really major investment drop, comparable to 1937 or to the first stages of the Great Depression, it can be seen that a compensatory public contribution of the order of $50 to $75 billion does not become fantastic.

In comparison with our past experience in government spending these are vast sums, and no one would be surprised if Congress faltered before such appropriations. It would undoubtedly seek to hold the dike with much smaller sums which, if they would not cure, would at least palliate the situation. Or it might try to reduce the scale of intervention by adopting policies which discouraged individual and corporate savings (and their necessary counterpart, investment), and which sought to make us a high-consumption or high-leisure economy.

But there is a price to be paid in both instances. A minimum program of "relief" might prevent serious social unrest—but it would not suffice to bring about continued expansion. And in the same fashion, a high-consumption economy might very well offer an excellent solution to the problem of instability, but it would also entail the abandonment of growth as an overriding economic objective. Investment may be the prime source of instability for our economy, but it is also the means by which growth is achieved. Hence if a rapid and continuing rise in our standard of living is to remain our main economic objective, we *must* have a high level of investment. And as an inescapable consequence, we must also be prepared to step in with a high level of compensatory spending if ever and whenever that investment fails.

7. *The Problem of the Public Subsector*

We are now in a better position to judge the prospects for our continued growth in the absence of an expanding military sector. For we can see that the critical question is not only whether the main forces of private enterprise will provide the necessary momentum. This is essentially an unanswerable question. It may be that private investment will give us all the impetus we need and that growth will materialize apace. What consequences would follow from this is a matter to which we shall shortly return. But there is at least the grave risk that spontaneous growth will not live up to expectations or desires. In that case, our continued expansion will hinge on our willingness to enlarge the boundaries of public spending far beyond what we now consider to be their "normal" extent.

This is a matter to which we have as yet paid little serious public attention. But if we have been able to sidestep the issue, it is not because it does not exist. It is because we *already have* a large planned sub-sector which we conveniently fail to recognize as such. This sector is, of course, our $45 billion core of military outlays.

However the fact that we already possess an important subsector of military expenditures does not yet dispose of the difficulties of developing a *non-military* sector by which it might be replaced in whole or in large part. We have heretofore only stressed the function of our present military expenditures in helping to sustain our forward momentum. Now we must pay heed to a second but no less useful purpose which they also play. This is the provision of channels through which large amounts of public funds can be spent without trespassing on the traditional areas of private activity.

For in many respects the defense sector is an "ideal" economic source of stimulation. Not only does much of its procurement reach down into the very heart of the nation's capital goods industries, such as aircraft, shipbuilding, steel, construction work, etc., but the goods which the defense effort brings forth in no way compete with or intrude upon the normal economy. The business of supplying military needs is business which would otherwise simply not exist. It is entirely extraneous to the demands of a civil economy and to the economic activity which would fulfill those demands. Thus by providing us with two immiscible economies—one public-military and one private-civilian—the defense sector enables us to gain the full benefits of a powerful government planning operation without actually confronting the problems of a true "mixed" economy.

But in the default of a defense sector—or in the event that the defense program levels off—the public stimulation of the economy, on a scale and with a directness of impact needed to start up the stalled motors of growth, would very likely encroach upon the limits of private activity. This is, for example, true of the repair and renewal of America's decaying cities, or the co-ordinated attack on its river valley development—two obvious candidates for massive public expenditure. One need only think of the opposition of the power companies to the present unambitious proposals for valley development, or the dogged resistance of real estate interests to every large urban renewal plan to imagine the opposition which would be called forth by a "socialistic" $50 billion program in these fields. Much the same difficulties would be likely to greet another use of public funds—their employment for a greatly expanded foreign aid program. Whether the American people would stand for the necessary billions of dollars worth of American goods being "given away" annually is in itself a debatable point. But, in any event, the public purchase of so sizable a fraction of American production as would be necessary to ensure our undiminished economic growth would again very probably call forth the specter of "socialism."

8. Plan or No Plan

There is, of course, reason for this fear. One cannot plan large government expenditures—not even, as we now do, for defense purposes—without diminishing to some extent the hegemony of private enterprise. Every enlargement of the government sector inevitably increases the area of "socialized" —i.e., public—activity at the expense of private activity. From this point of view, the movement into overt planning would unquestionably confirm the fact which our movement into covert planning conceals—that we are gradually shifting ever further away from traditional *laissez-faire* capitalism into a new structure of economic responsibilities.

Actually this is very far from saying that the need for planning portends the radical transformation of American capitalism. As in Europe, the main identifying features of capitalism are not apt to be much changed. The concentrated ownership of property, the profit motive, the market mechanism would certainly remain at the heart of the economy. If private enterprise remains buoyant—and this is the very purpose of planning—the government sector will very likely comprise little if any more than the 20 to 25 per cent of the economy *which it does now*. Although its activities will be more openly "civilian," more "socialistic," the aim of this limited planning will not be to undermine the surrounding main body of capitalism but to preserve it.

What gives weight to this conclusion is a highly significant difference between the over-all situation of American capitalism and that which is characteristic of so much of capitalism in Europe. In America, with negligibly few exceptions, the aspirations of the masses are *identified* with the prevailing order. There is here, as abroad, a pressure from below for more egalitarian income distribution, broader welfare benefits, etc. But these demands are all conceived and sought *within* the framework of the social system as it now exists. Socialism as an ideal is virtually nonexistent in America. Hence planning, as a social instrument, would tend to have a conservative rather than a radical aim.

This is not, however, the way it is apt to appear to many sections of the community. If the past offers any guide, it can be predicted with assurance that business will bitterly object to the emergence of an overt public investment subsector—particularly if it is planned on a scale commensurate with the large expenditures which may be necessary. Many other social groups, which have been indoctrinated with the belief that the public control of economic activity leads inevitably to the collectivization of other forms of life, will add their opposition to that of the industrial leaders. It is not impossible that the conservative elements in society would prefer to risk all, whatever fate might befall them in the advent of a really crushing depression, rather than surrender before the advance of a "hostile" ideology. Perhaps what they would most prefer would be for growth to take its own course—forging ahead when investment prospects opened up, and stagnating when they lacked, while an adequate program of "relief" prevented social morale from deteriorating unduly.

But such a "natural" condition of alternate growth and stagnation may become increasingly difficult to maintain. For in addition to our internal pressures, an external source of pressure also urges us powerfully in the direction of a publicly controlled economy. This is our competition with the Soviet Union.

The recent awakening to Russian technological and scientific parity with ourselves has come as a dramatic shock. But over the longer term future, it is likely to be far less shaking than our gradual awareness of the diminishing gap between Russian economic achievements and our own. As we have previously noted, the Russian over-all economy has been growing approximately twice as fast as our own; during the last recession it grew three times as fast. We are still far ahead of the Soviets in actual output. But it is only a matter of simple arithmetic to calculate that if the Soviet pace of advance and our own are both maintained, it will not be too many generations before Russia will rival us, not only in the production of steel and other basic industrial products but possibly even in general living standards. As a matter of fact, if our economy had failed to emerge from its recession, it would have been "overtaken"—in global figures—in less than fifteen years.

To many people—and particularly to our industrial leaders —this catching up of the Soviets is likely to be construed as a formidable challenge to the American economic system. Hence we already find in business and government circles a growing determination to match the Russian rate of growth— or at least to improve our own. When Khrushchev, in November, 1958, announced the new Seven Year Plan under which Russia's total output was scheduled to rise by 80 per cent, our instinctive reaction was that our prestige and power depended on raising our own rate of growth from the 4 per cent trend of the past decade to 5, 6, or even 7 per cent in the future. To continue at our then laggard economic pace, said Allen Dulles, was "virtually to commit economic suicide."

Whether an attempt to catch up with the Russian rate of growth constitutes an adequate answer to their historic challenge is a question which the protagonists of more rapid expansion rarely ask—just as they regularly fail to consider whether we *could* catch up without a considerable degree of economic planning. Regardless of these unanswered considerations, however, it seems certain that the narrowing gap with

Russia makes a prolonged absence of growth at home politically intolerable. The palliation of "temporary recessions,"
the mere marking of time while the economy seeks an adequate
channel for private expansion—these expedients of the past
are sure to seem less attractive as the Russians forge on ahead.
The patience of the unemployed, who waited through ten
years of the Great Depression for "normal conditions" to re-
appear, is a display of social docility not likely to be repeated.
Even from the conservative side the clamor for renewed expansion is apt to ring louder than the opposition to the "socialized" measures needed to bring it about.

As the conservative interest in re-expansion should make
clear, the trend to planning cannot be considered a scheme
being foisted upon us by "socialistic" thinkers. On the contrary, it is a defensive response of our society to the changed
environment of history with which it must contend. Essentially we are pushed in the direction of planning because
there is no other way of assuring growth in the advent of a
breakdown of private investment; and essentially we must
grow because we are likely to deem an absence of growth
to be a more dangerous threat to the prestige and power of
capitalism than its partial "socialization." At bottom it is not
an alien ideology which forces us into a new economic structure. It is self-preservation. Hard necessities of technology, of
public morale, of international competition relentlessly point
the way.

For a time, however, we can postpone, minimize, even deny
this impending realization. As long as our defense expenditures
continue to provide a channel for the constant stimulation of
vital industries, and as long as those expenditures continue to

grow, we can enjoy the benefits of a planned public sector while ignoring the fact that it exists. But unless our military budget is to rise indefinitely, sooner or later the issue must be faced. Then we shall have to recognize that, without preparation for public investment on a hitherto unimagined scale, the maintenance of our forward progress is likely to be fatally endangered.

Thus the meaningful alternatives which the future holds out are not those of plan or no plan. To insist doggedly upon the latter is to run the risk of grave social dislocation at home and loss of the ideological battle abroad. The question which is open and pregnant with meaning is what *kind* of planning, what *direction* of growth will best promote our chances for survival while preserving the values of an open society. It is on the answers to these questions, and not on a dogmatic refusal to consider them, that our social destiny will turn.

9. *The Embarras de Richesses*

Up to this point we have been engaged in examining the changes which may be necessary in the structure of the American economy if we are to translate the prospect of sustained vigorous growth into an actuality. Now we must look beyond the means to the end. We must ask not how growth can be attained, but what will be the effect of attaining it, regardless of whether it is gained by public investment or under the unaided aegis of private economic expansion. In a word, we must now inquire into the central economic characteristic of the American future as a determinant of its historic environment.

Many of the aspects of that environment we cannot foresee. What ideals and aspirations, what values and standards may characterize a society of abundance is largely a matter for conjecture. But one impending change we *can* anticipate, for it is wrapped up in the very meaning of abundance itself. This is a serious deterioration in our accustomed mechanism of social control.

It is one of the dangerous self-deceptions of our society to pretend that mechanisms of control do not really exist, and to maintain, without qualification, that we are an economically "free" people. In fact what we mean is that we are free in a number of extremely important ways, such as the right to choose our own employment. But, while esteeming our freedom, we must not let it blind us to a condition which permits it. After all, our economic liberty could result in a disastrous social breakdown if our free choices of employment left undone the tasks on which the community depends. We have but to imagine the consequences for a great metropolis— to take but a trivial example—if no one chose to become a subway worker or bus driver, to understand the danger inherent in economic freedom.

But the risk in real life is small. For the preceding condition to our economic freedom is the knowledge that the tasks *will* get done. And this knowledge comes to us not out of a respect for our intelligence or civic dutifulness, but because we know that *economic pressure will drive us to do them*. That is to say, when we ask how it is that free men go willingly to the subways or the busses, the assembly line or the office, the answer is: *There is where the jobs are;* and when we ask why free men charge so little—barely more than a modest comfort—to do work they do not much enjoy, the answer is: *They are not worth more*—which is to say that by virtue of their low levels of skill, their educational and cultural deficiencies, their lack of wealth, they are not able to strike too hard a bargain for doing what must be done.

This has been an eternal condition of society. But it is a condition which the emergence of abundance begins to undermine. For if the approach to abundance has any one paramount historic significance, it is the gradual elimination of a group hitherto so prevalent as to be beyond need of notice, and so indispensable as to be simply taken for granted—the great mass of anonymous men on whose generalized willingness to work the high edifices of civilization have been built. It is this group which abundance slowly causes to disappear. The diffusion of well-being down into the lower ranks of society gradually obliterates the line between those who have not and who must, and those who have and who therefore need not. Society is increasingly composed of those who need not.

In the immediate offing, the extension of economic well-being portends mainly a continuation of that trend toward equality of incomes which we have previously noted. That is, it promises a gradual drying-up of applicants for the meaner jobs of society, and the steady increase in pay for those who will still take them. But somewhat more distantly a still more disturbing prospect appears. This is the possibility that as the level of general affluence reaches upper-middle-class levels there may be *no* arrangement of incomes or rewards which will lure men to the posts society must fill. England experienced a foretaste of such an impasse in the postwar period, when its miners began to use their new-found affluence to leave the pits. By 1952 the number of boys and young men in the mines, which a generation before totaled over 150,000, had dwindled to less than 50,000. In desperation, miners' wages, which had been as low as eightieth on the scale of industrial pay, were raised to head the list. Amenities of many kinds were introduced by the National Coal Board. Both the miners' union and the Socialist government urged the miners to remain in the industry. Nonetheless the efflux continued. In the end, England had to import foreign miners to maintain an adequate force at the coal face.

We have encountered a similar efflux from "dirty work" at home, although in somewhat disguised form. We must ask ourselves where our society would recruit its menial workers— its domestics, elevator men, janitors, dishwashers, heavy laborers—if we did not possess a pool of "foreign" labor in our Negro, Mexican, Puerto Rican, and other ethnic minorities. At a higher level, despite the fact that factory jobs pay better —often far better—than clerical jobs, the sons of the middle class do not follow the arrow of economic advantage: they want "more" from a job than "just" pay. Tomorrow, when this class is even more ubiquitous, we may feel the acute lack of a labor force which seeks no index to a job except its pay. In a society of general abundance, even very high wages are not apt to tempt men to jobs which they do not associate with status and dignity.

No doubt such a condition of general economic independence is admirable. Certainly it is preferable to the situation that obtains today where freedom accrues to those who have wealth and necessity weighs upon those who do not. But independence must nonetheless be made compatible with the continuity of the human community itself. If the pressure of economic need, which already barely suffices to fill every chamber of the social engine, should fall far enough, that engine will halt.

All these portents point in one direction. *They signify that the price of an economy of abundance is the replacement of the traditional economic control mechanism with new kinds of social controls.* The central problem of the new society will be to find the means of assuring its own discipline in place of the disappearing force of economic pressure.

This conclusion, which is most apparent in the case of "dirty work," is reinforced many-fold when we extend the consequences of diminishing economic pressure to the economy at large. For we can then see that the traditional means of control over *business* as well as over labor are being eroded by the waning of economic necessity.

Historically, that control was exercised by the mechanism of the competitive market—a mechanism which imposed upon business enterprises the same obedience to the "social will" as it did upon labor. But just as the market exerted its effective discipline upon labor through the pressure of economic necessity, so did it impose its commands upon business with an imperious force based upon the necessity of economic survival. Businesses which failed to compete ruthlessly, which put conscience above profit-seeking, which disregarded the demands of the market place, were simply eliminated from the system.

It is hardly necessary to point out that these stringent requirements for survival have been considerably weakened, particularly in the central bastions of the economy. The cutthroat competition which still characterized the industrial battles of the late nineteenth century has largely given way to the live-and-let-live competition of "customer service" under the protective cover of administered—i.e., non-competing—prices. The merciless quest for business profit, which provided the main criterion for management in the past, is being replaced or supplemented, as business itself continually asserts, by wider considerations, such as business' "obligations" to the community. All this no doubt testifies in the first instance to the growing power and perhaps conscience of giant firms. But it is also tacit proof that business no longer *has to* engage in a dog-eat-dog struggle in order to survive.

Equally significant is the growth of another characteristic of business behavior—its manipulation and creation of consumer demand through advertising. This much-observed phenomenon is commonly deplored for its socially deleterious effects. But what escapes notice is that this behavior, too, reflects a weakening of the strictures of economic necessity. In the nineteenth century, as Professor Galbraith has remarked, no one needed an advertising man to tell him what he wanted. If today the consumer is more and more the creature of advertising, the fault does not reside in the malicious intentions of business. It lies in the fact that with the rise of abundance the nature of consumer demand has radically changed. It is no longer concentrated on the basic necessities of life, as was the case in a time of prevailing low standards of life. More and more the purchasing "power" of an abundant society is unformulated in character, evidencing itself only in a general willingness to spend large sums on any number of possible goods. In the demand for cars, television sets, air conditioners, and the like, there are no more patterns of exigent need, but only diffuse and capricious desires; and these desires, rather than imposing their "will" unambiguously on business, naturally invite the imposition of business' will upon themselves. Indeed business is forced to create and capture the public will if it is to have any reasonable assurance of stability in the "wants" to which it caters.[10]

In more or less dramatic fashion all these aspects of big business behavior reflect the weakening of the imperious economic pressures which once enforced the "rules" of traditional market behavior. But there is more at stake than a change in economic manners. What is crucial in the loosening of the market mechanism is the gradual disappearance of the traditional means of *social control* over business. With the slackening of the pressures of economic necessity, the very preconditions for the market regulation of economic activity are slowly vitiated. Business is no longer subservient to the market, but the market becomes more and more subservient to business. As a result the ultimate direction of economic affairs passes

[10] I am indebted for this point to Dr. Adolph Lowe. See also his comment on "The Practical Uses of Theory," *Social Research*, Summer, 1959. For changed market behavior see J. K. Galbraith, *American Capitalism* and *The Affluent Society* (Boston, 1952 and 1958). Cf. also Ben Lewis, "Economics by Admonition," Am. Ec. Assoc., *Papers & Proceedings*, May, 1959, esp. pp. 395-97.

from society at large to the centers of business (and labor) power.

We are as yet only in the initial stages of this breaking down of the traditional mechanisms of control. No doubt for some time the accustomed market pressures will serve their purposes well enough. But it is already clear in respect to both labor and business that the drive toward abundance is creating a vacuum in the established means of socio-economic control. Over the next decades the inherent effects of abundance are certain to make that lack of discipline more serious. Gradually the taskmaster of necessity is being displaced, and as a result the lines of command over labor and business are weakening. Unless society is to deliver itself into the hands, benign or otherwise, of these authorities, another taskmaster will have to be found.

What that source of social discipline might be is a speculative matter. The measures which may be needed to re-establish social control over business, the degree of compulsion which may be required to allocate labor, the range of economic freedom, as we know it, permissible in a society which lacks an "invisible hand"—these are all questions of great moment but unanswerable complexity. It may be that in the end the loss will outweigh the gain, and that we shall acquire economic abundance only at the cost of crushing social restrictions. Yet there can be no turning back from a prospect whose material allurements far exceed these premonitions of future constraint. Nor, perhaps, should there be. The important thing, rather, is to realize that the road to abundance leads subtly but surely into the society of control. It is not too early to consider the kind of society that might be.

10. *The Mastery of Technology*

These prospects for the future throw a light upon the historic trend of the American economy different from that in which we are accustomed to seeing it. But we have yet to place our economic momentum in one final and decisive perspective. We have been considering the long-term implications of growth as an isolated phenomenon. Now we must view that growth in the context of the transformations which surround it—the increasing penetration of science and technology, the violent emergence into world history of the underdeveloped countries, the worldwide retreat from capitalism.

When we begin to consider our economic momentum in this context, one relationship suggests itself immediately. This is the intimate—indeed, the inseparable—connection between our economic expansion and the scientific and technological character of our civilization. As we have seen, our growth is not only largely dependent on the upward curve of invention and discovery, but it becomes an economic reality by adding layer upon layer of technical apparatus to the productive foundation of the economy. Thus the very assumption of economic growth implies an enormous addition to the complexity and the sheer mass of our technological underpinnings.

What precise form the technology of the future may take, we do not know. But we can at least observe the salient directions in which industrial development is moving. One such direction, in which we have barely begun to explore, is the widespread automation of industry. Another is the mechanization, not of factory work, but of the simplest and most traditional tasks within the home. Yet another, still further removed from the industrial base, is the refinement of the arts of communication and persuasion. These general avenues of advance, diverse as they are, nonetheless present a common aspect to the private person. In one fashion or another, they weaken his solitary capacity to cope with life, whether as a job-seeker faced with the threat of technological displacement, or as a home-owner unable to make the most elementary repairs on his personal equipment without outside assistance, or as an individual mind treated as part of a mass audience. All impel the individual to define his existence in terms of an ever wider, more demanding engagement with his society. And this effect can be demonstrated in virtually every aspect of life with which modern technology comes into contact.

To a large extent this loss of personal mastery is an inescapable—and perhaps an increasing—condition of an age in which science has progressed far beyond the reach of any but the most highly trained minds. But what is at stake is not only a loss of personal mastery, of intellectual grasp. It is a loss of social mastery, of control over our own habitat. We are in the unpleasant position of watching our *society* change under the impact of its own technology while we stand impotently by to suffer the consequences for better or worse. And this loss of social mastery cannot be blamed only on the complexity of the technological process. It also lies with the fact that the main control we exercise over the social incursion of technology is that of economics.

It is at this point that our economic growth comes directly into contact with the historic shaping of the age of science. For our growth not only rests on technological advance, but is itself the regulator of the entrance of technology into our social system. We all realize that the speed with which automation will be introduced depends primarily on the *economic* advantages which it will bring, and that the main use of television is that which best lends itself to economic exploitation. In similar fashion, the rate at which the mechanical duplication of human skills is integrated into our homes likewise rests with the salability of the relevant devices. In a word, with few exceptions, we allow the products of science and technology, like half-tamed genii from Aladdin's lamp, to work their social will without hindrance, so long as they are economically obedient. As a result our economic growth steadily adds to our social involvement in technology in a manner which is essentially capricious and haphazard. We have narrowed our control over the incursion of scientific technology into our lives to the main and often to the single criterion of its profitability.

Three centuries ago, when industrial technology first loomed large on the social landscape, this narrowing of control had its rationale. For then the historic justification of technology was its promise of a great escape from poverty. With such an end in mind, it was indeed understandable that whatever products or processes commended themselves to the market place thereby confirmed their ultimate validity. Yet even with this overwhelming justification, the indiscriminate guidance of technology by the laws of economic advantage was very nearly fatal to capitalism. Industrial progress did finally engineer the great escape. But in the process of forming the basis for a new and more abundant society it simultaneously deformed and stunted much of the life for which that abundance was intended.

However compelling the rationale of economic control over technology three centuries ago, the same can hardly be said to apply today. The escape from poverty, at least in this country, has been largely completed. With a few signal exceptions, primary among which are medical research and the basic quest for scientific knowledge itself, the main flow of the scientific and technological effort associated with our economic momentum can scarcely be dignified as having for its purpose the fundamental elevation of the human estate.

Yet it continues to be of pressing human and social consequence. Whatever the purposes of the end products of industry, their ramification continues to refashion our lives—as workers and consumers, as economic citizens, as social beings. The products of industry may be less and less connected with the alleviation of poverty or of inhuman toil, but they are not less connected with the tempo and texture of social life. Meanwhile the processes of industry continue to socialize our existences, and only too late, when their effects have become visible in social conformity or a multiplication of the needs of government, do we object to what is "going on." But by then any possibility of intervening in the process of change is limited to a partial compensation for changes which have already been irreversibly fixed into place.

Much of this progressive socialization of our lives will continue no matter what. It is in the very nature of a scientific technology that it steadily contracts the boundaries of the self-sufficient person while expanding those of the public particle. But this inescapable consequence of our industrial civilization need not be a wholly blind process. The problem is not how to avoid the incursion of science and technology, but how to bring that incursion, with all its social consequences, under deliberate social control. In the end the question is: Who is to be master, man or his machines? As long as the control over technology rests primarily on economic calculation, the victor is not likely to be man.

11. *The Wrath of Nations*

We turn now to a second critical problem in which our growth involves us. This is our relationship to the underdeveloped world. And here we shall find, as with our encounter with the technological forces of our times, that the direction of our present economic momentum does not lead us away from the historic difficulties that this problem presents, but directly into the closest entanglement with them.

The problem can be succinctly recapitulated. The forces of modern history—technological, political, economic—are bringing the continents of the earth together in a fiercely compressing vise. China is now less than a day's flight away from us; soon it will be but a few hours. India is a vital and exposed bastion of Western political ideas; the Near East an indispensable part of the Western economic fortress. But this compression of the world is not only manifest from *our* side, as our inextricable involvement with the fate of the great masses of the world. Even more significant is the reality of the world's compression from *their* side, as the masses awaken to their existence as human beings on the same earth as ourselves.

As a result what was once a gulf which divided two wholly separate worlds is rapidly becoming a rift which divides one self-conscious human community. With each painful step forward, the peoples of the world become more alive to the conditions of humanity in countries other than their own. And of all these conditions the one which stands out is the terrible disparity of living conditions in their own lands compared with the lands of a favored few. The division of the world into the abjectly poor and the grossly rich—a condition of which the poor were always dimly aware, but which appeared as a matter of immutable fate, as an inscrutable destiny—suddenly becomes a dispensation of human history which seems iniquitous, intolerable, and infuriating. Their economic development, their catching up, becomes not just a matter of social policy, but of social justice.

But will they catch up? Dr. G. L. Bach, of the Carnegie Institute of Technology, writes of the prospects for Latin-American progress:

If we make the highly optimistic assumption that total Latin-American output will . . . provide a 2.5 percent annual growth in output per capita, it would still be some forty years before Latin-American per capita income reached one-third the *present* U.S. per capita income. But if U.S. income continues to grow at around two percent per year, it would be over 250 years before Latin-American income would reach one-third of the then-current United States income levels. Even if Latin-American per capita income rose at four percent a year, more than fifty years would be required to reach one-third of the then prevailing U.S. levels.[11]

It is not difficult to project the effect of a race in which the poorer nations would watch the richer draw steadily ahead of them, or in which after their vast labors they would find the gap in no wise diminished. It would expose us to a wrath and fury of a kind we have never heretofore known—a *proletarian* wrath.

Yet this is precisely what is betokened as the outcome of our present economic thrust. It is now our proud—and sometimes our proudest—boast that with but 6 per cent of the world's population we produce 40 per cent of its goods. If our desired trend of future growth materializes, that proportion—or disproportion—will remain roughly constant. Taking the various rates of growth as they exist in the world today, we would then find the gap between our living standards and those of Russia and China to be diminishing. But the distance between ourselves and the non-communist underdeveloped world would be *expanding*. For if Russia is today growing

[11] G. L. Bach, *Economics, An Introduction to Analysis and Policy* (New York, 1958), p. 806.

roughly twice as fast as we, we are growing at least twice as fast as India, most of South and Central America, and Africa.

This is clearly a prospect laden with the most dangerous consequences. Yet its remedy is by no means a simple one. We have already touched on the question of whether it would be politically feasible to mount a large and sustained foreign-assistance program—one which was measured in the requisite billions of dollars a year. But to the obvious difficulties of persuading the electorate of the desirability of such a program must be added the problem of our own reaction to the achievement of rapid growth in the underdeveloped areas. We have seen how much of the world has had to resort to an iron collectivism to break through the inertia of the past. To bring about comparable rates of economic development in non-communist countries will require not only economic efforts of comparable intensity, but very likely social and political transformations of a far-reaching kind. In some nations, like Saudi Arabia (which has been described by one authority as "rushing madly from the eleventh century into the twelfth"), such transformations are likely to require a revolutionary upheaval.[12] In other nations, such as India or South America, they will require a degree of social enlistment, of political dedication, of economic marshaling of resources far beyond anything which has yet been manifested. Many of these revolutions or near-revolutions will be undemocratic. Most will take the form of a thoroughgoing socialism. All will take its name.

This places us on the horns of a tragic dilemma. On the one hand, it holds out the uncongenial prospect of a sharp left-

[12] From E. Mason, *Economic Planning in Underdeveloped Areas* (New York, 1958), p. 19.

ward and collectivist movement as the price of a steep upward economic ascent. On the other hand, it confronts us with the risk of an explosion of proletarian anger if, in the absence of such a movement, the gap between us and the non-communist world continues to widen.

In this prospect of bitter alternatives we have hitherto chosen to accept the risks of the second course. We have preferred to let foreign economic development lag, rather than to stir up the brew of social upheaval. In some nations, particularly in the Near East, we have lent support to governments which are anachronistic and corrupt, and which have a vested interest in *preventing* social advance. In others, our contribution to economic development has been grudging or none at all. Over the three years 1955–57, our total expenditures for the encouragement of growth for the peoples of India, Indonesia, South America, and Africa was one tenth of one per cent of our total gross national product. Prior to that it was less. As a result, in no backward nation in the world are we responsible for the commencement of an ascent in any degree comparable to those which are taking place under communist guidance.

This is surely a policy which will one day reap the whirlwind. And yet it is a policy born out largely of an unwillingness to face up to the fact that the alternatives *are* bitter. We find ourselves horrified and shocked by the social mechanics of forced economic progress, but unable as yet to contemplate the eventual consequences of a failure of this painful and perilous climb to take place.

It would be a grave error to oversimplify this tangled problem and to paint its aspects in clear whites and blacks. We have already cautioned against the bland hope that development, by itself, will usher in a period of stability and reasonableness when it may very well at first do the opposite. Yet in the longer view, if there is any hope for a convergence of views and attitudes, values and ideals, within the concert of nations, it must await some closure of the economic fissure which now divides the world. The coexistence of great riches and fearful poverty in a world community increasingly aware of its overarching human fraternity will, unless repaired, lead to eventual consequences as terrible as it did in the past, in those nations where rich and poor drew ever further apart.

12. *The Deepening Confusion*

Our analysis has revealed a disconcerting and even dismaying prospect. It is that economic growth, as a history-shaping force, tends not to alleviate the pressures of the constricting environment of the future, but to augment and aggravate those pressures. This does not mean that economic growth will not bring to millions of families a sense of wider horizons and greater individual well-being. It is not in order to deny the value and benefits of growth that our argument has unfolded, but to make it clear that growth is not simply a process by which we put a magnifying glass over the present. It is essentially and fundamentally a process of *change;* and the alternative it offers us is whether we will attempt to control that change, or permit it to obey its own internal economic momentum.

In all probability we shall follow the latter course. The most likely outlook is that things will go on much as they are. To begin now to establish those non-economic motives and incentives which might later ease the problem of control of a society of abundance would be to interfere seriously with the present incentive system. To subject our technological development to non-economic control, would be to take out of the hands of business one of its primary "rights." To embark on an aggressive policy of foreign economic development would require a radical readjustment of prevailing ideas about the role and prospects for private enterprise in the developing world. All these changes would drastically curtail the established hegemony and prerogatives of business power. They would substantially shrink the boundaries of private enterprise, and very greatly enlarge the boundaries of the public authority. The amalgam would be, if not socialist by the traditional definitions, far closer to socialism than we are today.

It is certain that such a rearrangement of economic responsibilities would be fiercely resisted by the business community. What is more important, in all likelihood it would also find little if any support from the other sectors of society. Popular sentiment today allies itself with the centers of economic power in the view that the future lies with the maximum unrestricted growth of our economic capacity. The average American family, engrossed in its present needs and understandably desirous of material advance, is not much exercised over changes which seem remote, nebulous, and far from the realities of daily life. As much as or more than the business community, it abides by the belief that abundance will simply make life easier without reflecting on its associated problems which also make it more difficult; that uncontrolled technological change will bring "miracles" into our lives but exact no price for them; that our proper response to the narrowing of the gap with the communist nations is to run all the faster, regardless of the effect on the non-communist world. From top to bottom America is prepared to let these aspects of "history" take care of themselves. And so, of course, they will.

Hence what seems to lie ahead is a slow, largely imperceptible but gradually cumulating trend in the general directions we have seen. No doubt the initial battle will have to be fought over the means of assuring the growth we desire, and of replacing our present covert planning with an overt acceptance of its necessity. Thereafter, if our growth is successfully achieved, we can expect an intensification of those economic and social pressures which stem from the upward revaluation of labor in a society of growing abundance. Still some distance ahead lies the graver problem of staffing the posts and controlling the productive institutions of a system in which the pressures of necessity have given way to the "freedom" of a society of abundance. Whether, forty years hence, when our economy can yield an average family an income of $10,000, we shall be able to maintain over-all control by the traditional economic incentives is a matter of real doubt, and—for those who fear the growth of the state as an authoritarian instrument —of very real concern. How, in much less than forty years, our increasingly independent centers of business power will be made responsive to some public control other than their self-manipulated markets and their own consciences may be an even more crucial problem.

Meanwhile we must also anticipate a further rise of the impotence and incompetence of the individual vis-à-vis the social environment which modern technology creates. In the factory and in the home, in his cities and as a national citizen in his land, the individual will find himself increasingly forced to adapt to technological changes whose advent he did not order but must nonetheless accept, whose operation is beyond him, and whose ultimate impact he does not understand. This in turn implies a further growth of the private and public bureaucracies which control the complex whole and which support the dependent human being.

Finally the future holds out the grave threat of an ideological isolation of the American system. In this regard it is instructive and sobering for us to reflect on the case of England. Having won an empire "in a fit of absent-mindedness," sincerely convinced of the enlightenment of their motives and of their dedication to the cause of liberty, the English found it difficult to believe that so much of the colonial world regarded their nation as a sinister power. In much the same fashion it is difficult for us, who are absent-mindedly creating our own civilization and who are convinced of the purity of our international motives, to believe that much of the world sees us as a malign and threatening influence.

Vis-à-vis Europe it is likely that a common heritage of values and a growing convergence of economic structures can prevent what would truly be a tragic ideological rift. The matter is not so easily reconciled, however, when we assess the situation in relation to the poorer lands to East and South. One can hope for a growth of mutual sympathy and understanding—on our part, for the problems and urgency of development, and on the part of the developing nations, for the relevance of political and intellectual freedom even in an age of radical change. But we would be ill-advised to ignore the possibility that an excess of lavish growth at home, coupled with an ideological rigidity abroad, may turn the hostility of a starving and frustrated world against us.

It must be evident that these challenges are of the utmost seriousness for the long-run survival of the kind of society we are. Yet few of the portending developments have an air of immediate crisis. Only gradually and obscurely will the incremental changes in the environment assume clear outlines or display their full force. For a considerable time it will be possible for America to believe that by its unrestrained growth it is posing an effective counterchallenge to the closing-in of history.

But as the future unfolds, it is clear that this counterchallenge will provide less and less of an "answer" to the problems of the emerging environment. For it is certain that the future will bring realities for which our traditional optimism fails to prepare us and against which our economic momentum fails to arm us. In this state of unreadiness before the advent of history, it is not catastrophe or collapse which impends. Rather it is an exacerbation of the mood which already assails us—an unhappy disarray of purposes, a cloudy outlook, a dismay at the untoward drift of events. What we may be able to do in the face of this deepening confusion is a matter to which we shall turn in our next chapter. But it must be evident we cannot even begin to hope that our response will be adequate so long as we fail to see that the very counterchallenge which we have posed to the historic constriction of our times contains profound and inescapable challenges of its own.

IV

⇢》《⇠

THE
FUTURE
AS
HISTORY

1. *A Recapitulation*

In our last two chapters we have been concerned with the great currents by which the future environment is being shaped and formed. Now it is time to step back, and in the light of the historic outlook, to consider again a question with which we began our investigations. This is our *state of mind* about the future—the philosophy of expectations with which we orient ourselves to its challenges, and beyond them, to the sweep of history itself.

In the past, as we know, we have approached the future with the sustaining beliefs of a philosophy of optimism. That is, we have always conceived of the future in terms of its benignity, its malleability, its compatibility with our hopes and desires. But if our preceding pages have had any purpose, it has been to demonstrate the inadequacy of this belief today. It is no longer possible for America to commit itself trustingly into the hands of a deity of history whose agent forces are comfortably circumscribed and comfortingly familiar. If one thing is certain it is that history's forces have reached a power utterly unlike that of our sheltered past, and that the changes those forces portend are very different from the propitious historic transformations they brought about in our past.

Let us briefly recapitulate what some of those changes are likely to be:

1. As a consequence of the new weapons technology we have not only lost our accustomed military security, but also any possibility of enforcing a military "solution" to the problem of communism. The weapons stalemate has thus magnified the influence of the non-military determinants of the central struggle of our times. The "historic forces" of politics and economics, of technologies and ideologies, are therefore of crucial importance in the resolution of this contest.

2. The trend of these forces is not an encouraging one. In the huge continents to the East and South we have witnessed an explosive awakening of hitherto ignored or abused peoples, who now seek a rapid redress of their age-old grievances. This has led the underdeveloped nations into a desperate effort for economic development—an effort which, in the environment of underdevelopment, turns naturally in the direction of economic collectivism. There are strong possibilities that this collectivism will veer far to the left, whether or not it falls directly under communist hegemony. It is likely as well to discard the frail structures of democracy, and to maintain its morale by an exaggerated nationalism. Finally, we must not ignore the possibility that American economic growth, by widening the gap between the underdeveloped peoples and ourselves, may place America at the focus of the frustration and resentments which economic development is likely at first to generate.

3. At the same time, the drift of Western society is itself away from the traditional forms of capitalism. In all nations,

including our own, a framework of "socialist" planning is replacing the unregulated market mechanism. In Europe this drift into planning is made more significant by the fact that European capitalism, unlike American, is not a self-assured and unchallenged social order.

4. However, within our own nation there are strong tendencies which move us away from the traditional, and now perhaps nostalgic idea of American society. One of these is the rampant technological and scientific development which marks our time. This development manifests itself in a proliferation of institutions needed to "support" the increasingly dependent individual, and in the rise of bureaucratic apparatuses needed to control the technological machinery itself. The rise of the welfare state, on the one hand, and of the military bureaucracy, on the other, are instances of the manner in which technology is enforcing a socialization of life.

5. There are also visible other tendencies which are transforming our society, particularly in its economic aspect. There is a strong likelihood that a radical redefinition of the limits of public economic activity will be enforced by the pressure of events. Over the near future this is likely to be provided in disguised form by the enlarging military sector, but in the longer run we shall probably be forced to find civilian outlets to replace the military. Somewhat further ahead lies the still more difficult problem of providing internal economic discipline in a society in which the usual market control mechanisms are increasingly weakened by widespread social abundance.

6. All these collectivist trends are accelerated by our main historic movement—our growth. The problem then is the degree to which our blind economic momentum makes it impossible to respond effectively to the technological, political, and economic forces which are bringing about a closing-in of our historic future. This is a question to which dogmatic answers cannot be given. But it must be pointed out that an effective control over the historic forces of our times would require changes not only in the structure of power but in the common denominator of values, which do not seem likely to occur, at least for a considerable period.

The probabilities, in other words, are that "history" will go against us for a long time, and that the trend of events, both at home and abroad, will persist in directions which we find inimical and uncongenial. It would be foolish to pretend to a degree of prescience about the future which no amount of analysis can provide, or to be doctrinaire about the evolution of events. Yet surely, to hope for the best in a situation where every indication leads us to expect a worsening, is hardly the way to fortify ourselves against the future. Optimism as a philosophy of historic expectations can no longer be considered a national virtue. It has become a dangerous national delusion.

But if our optimism fails and misleads us, what shall we put in its place? How shall we prepare ourselves for the oncoming challenges of the future? What might be the character of a philosophy suited to our times? These are the deeply meaningful questions to which we now turn.

2. *The Failures of Optimism*

It may help us to formulate answers to these questions if we ask ourselves what it has been about the recent past for which optimism as a philosophy of historic expectations has failed to prepare us. The answer is explicit in the theme of this book. It is an outlook on the future *as history*.

This is not to say that optimism does not contain—albeit tacitly—an estimate of the future "as history." We have already endeavored to show its roots in the technological, political, and economic forces that have generated modern history, and its unconscious assumptions about the automatic progress which those forces effect. But what is missing from the philosophy of optimism is a conscious recognition of the special circumstances of history from which it arose and about which it generalizes. It is a failure to see itself as the product of a unique and sheltered historic experience which could not be enlarged into a model for all historic experience irrespective of its setting.

As a result, optimism has misled us in two particulars. First, it has caused us to overestimate the degree of our freedom in history. Because it mirrors an historic experience in which our conscious efforts to "make" history coincided with and were aided by the movement *of* history, optimism has given us the notion that history is only, or largely, the product of our volitions. Thus it has deluded us as to our power when the forces of history run not with, but counter to, our designs. It has filled us with a belief that everything is possible, and has made it not a sign of wisdom but a suspicion of weakness to think in terms of what is impossible.

Secondly, optimism has given us a simplistic idea of the forces of history. Assessing those forces in terms of their eighteenth- and nineteenth-century manifestations, it has failed to alert us to the possibility that the identical basic forces, in another environment, might lead to very different results from those which we assume to be their natural outcome. Thus the philosophy of optimism has presented the idea of technical progress solely in terms of the enhancement of man's productive powers—which was indeed its outstanding attribute in the past—rather than in terms of the social repercussions of technology which may well be its principal impact upon us in the present and future. Similarly, the optimistic outlook has taught us that the impetus of popular political aspiration leads naturally to the development of democratic governments, as it did in the cradle of history in which it was nurtured, but has failed to alert us as to the turning which those self-same aspirations can take—and have already taken—in an environment in which the preconditions for Western parliamentary democracy are totally absent. Finally, in the terms of the optimistic philosophy, the consequences of economic progress have been perhaps the most artlessly conceived of all. Quite aside from whether it correctly judged the outcome of the internal mechanics of capitalism, the optimistic outlook made economic advancement itself an unambiguous and self-evident social goal—a point of view which, however justified by the conditions of insufficiency of the nineteenth century, entirely obscures the new problems, both of organization and of values, which the achievement of abundance itself brings into being.

Thus if we are to suggest the attributes of a philosophy of expectations better adapted to our times than that of optimism, we shall have to explore more fully the two main areas in which optimism is deficient. First we shall have to ask: What is possible at this moment in our history? What are the limits of intervention into, what are the "necessities" of the historic process? Secondly, we shall have to inquire: What attributes of the forces of history are neglected by the philosophy of optimism? How can we prepare for their unexpected and often unwelcome repercussions? In a word, how can we think about the future as history?

3. The Limits of the Possible

Everyone who considers the first of these questions—what is "possible" and "impossible" in history—soon comes up against a classic dilemma. This is the dilemma of "free will"— or in terms of the historic process, of determinism versus historic freedom. It is the dilemma of choosing between a world where everything is "possible" and therefore where nothing can be counted on, including the most basic necessities for the continuance of the human community; and a world where nothing is possible, and therefore where nothing can be hoped for except that which is inevitably and immutably fixed and beyond alteration. It is a choice between history as chaos and history as a prison.

This is a dilemma which still exercises philosophers and historians. But the dilemma has more to do with the limitations of abstract thought than with the experience of history itself. For when we turn to the living reality of history, we do not encounter a dilemma, but a *problem*—which is a very different thing. And this problem is not to formulate the meaning of historic freedom in general and forever, but to determine in the light of the actualities of the moment how much of history lies within our grasp and how much lies beyond.

Once we approach the matter in this direct and pragmatic fashion, the idea of what is "possible" in history presents itself intelligibly enough before us. We then find ourselves confronted, as a condition of life, with a situation which may be logically awkward but which is not at all awkward as a fact. This is the coexistence of freedom and necessity in history— the simultaneous existence of its glacial imperturbability, its "laws," its "necessities" on the one hand, and its "freedom," its openness, its amenability to our wills on the other.

The point at which we can divide freedom from necessity also comes to us with reasonable clarity. We all know that there are some historic events—such as, for instance, the internal politics of Soviet rule—which it is virtually impossible for us to affect. We recognize another class of events that lie directly—or at least to an important degree—within the scope of our control and responsibility. The "possibility" of war, for instance, is a matter in which we are quite sure that our free decisions play an immense and probably determinative role—all the more so, since so many aspects of the "historic" situation clearly set the stage for war.

This is, however, only one way of assessing what is historically possible for us. For what we deem to be "historic events" by no means exhausts the aspects of change and development in history. As Karl Popper reminds us, "There is no history of mankind, there is only an indefinite number of histories of all kinds of aspects of human life";[1] and when we turn to those aspects of history with which this book has been primarily concerned—the aspects of social change rather than of immediate political conflict—we find our possibilities of history-making sharply curtailed. In our society, the "history" of technological progress and penetration, or the "history" of political belief and economic development are not facets of human life which we normally subject to "history-making" decisions. In general we allow these aspects of history to follow their autonomous courses, and to evolve by their unguided interactions. Thus we limit our idea of what is possible in history by excluding from our control the forces of history themselves.

This is a very different situation from that which obtains in a more collectivistic society. The enormous national effort of Russian growth or the wholesale alterations in the social structure of China are instances of historic change whose

[1] *The Open Society* (London, 1952), vol. II, p. 270.

possibility was initially discounted by observers who had in mind the limitations of historic intervention in our own kind of society. The point, then, is that there are no fixed and immutable limits to what is historically possible. Rather, different organizations of society define for themselves the limits of what is and what is not within reach of conscious history-making choice. Authoritarian societies, as a generality, have a much more comprehensive direction of the "forces" of history than open societies. On the other hand, open societies, through their democratic apparatus, retain a wider degree of control over the course of their "heroic" history, i.e., over the policies of their leaders.

4.   *The Possibilities Before America*

What does this imply for the "possibility" of altering the historic outlook that lies before us?

To the extent that we are concerned with those aspects of the future which will be molded by the anonymous forces of technology, political ideology, and economic evolution, we must accept the conclusion that the possibilities of major intervention are not great. For the portents of the future spring, in the main, from underlying pressures of ideologies and from the fixed structures of institutions whose conscious manipulation does not now lie within the reach of our accepted "history-making" powers. Of course we can make small changes in the superstructure of our institutions. But if, for example, we really want to undo the "creeping socialism" of our time, we should have to do more than legislate away our institutions of social welfare and economic control. To remove these institutions without removing the massive technology and the economic instability which have produced them would only be to open the way for a social explosion which would probably swing even further leftward. Essentially, the only way to halt the creep of "socialism" is to return to an atomistic economy with small-scale technical and economic units, and with a wholly different climate of political and social beliefs. This it is obviously impossible for us to attempt, without a degree of historic intervention which is entirely alien to our social philosophy.

It may even be that with the most violent assault upon "history," with the most revolutionary intervention into institutions and ideologies, it would still not be possible to reverse the basic direction of our historic momentum. In our time, we have seen extraordinary attempts to reshape the social forces of history, and extraordinary results in imposing a heroic, revolutionary will upon social history.[2] Yet the changes which were inaugurated were in nearly every instance in accord with the drift and temper of world history as a whole. There has been no successful revolution against the forces of technology, of popular political aspiration, and of socialism, although it is obvious that the slogans of "democ-

[2] For an excellent discussion of this problem in general, cf. Sidney Hook, *The Hero in History* (Boston, 1943), esp. Chap. XII.

racy" and "socialism" have been put to cruel use. No revolutionary has been able to preach anti-industrialism, or the inequality of classes, or the ideals of capitalism. Gandhi, who came closest to being an exception insofar as his dislike of technology was concerned, was nonetheless unable to keep India closed off from modern technology. The few nations which have sought to stand against the political trend—like Spain—have been in a state of exhaustion and have had no subsequent important historic development. There have been few major revolutions since 1945 which have not flown the banners of socialism.

Thus there seems indeed to be a basic character to world civilization in our times from which no vital historic effort can depart very far in its essentials, and the fact that even revolutions have had to conform to this pattern makes it unlikely in the extreme that a non-revolutionary society, such as our own, will succeed in resisting it. To what ultimate ends this "inevitable" direction of historic forces may carry society we do not know, for such questions take us far beyond the horizon of the "given" historic situation. What may be the final impact of science and technology on civilization, the end effect of our egalitarian political ideals, or the ultimate organization of collectivism, we do not know. All that we do know is that, for the moment, these general historic tendencies are firmly in the saddle, and that short of the profoundest change in the character of our civilization, or an incalculable redirection of events, they bid fair to dominate the social environment of the future.

But the fact that the *main direction* of historic movement is too deeply rooted to be turned aside does not mean that our future is therefore caught in a deterministic vise. It is not just necessity, but a mixture of necessity and freedom which, as always, confronts us as a condition of historic existence. If the idea of the future as history tells us what it is not "possible" for our kind of society to do, it also makes clear what *is* possible.

For example, the spreading hegemony of scientific technology may be an inescapable general tendency of our times, but the social consequences which we have previously discussed do not follow as an inescapable corollary. They are largely the result of *non-intervention* before the historic closing-in of science and technology. But non-intervention is not the only possible response to this historic force. It is rather a kind of abdication before the problem itself. It leads us to ignore the very thought that there may exist other controls over the technological revolution than the economic calculus which is at present our main device for regulating its admission into our lives. One need hardly say that a society which consistently ignored considerations of economics would seriously jeopardize its own well-being. But this does not mean that a society cannot, however imperfectly, attempt to weigh the non-economic advantages and disadvantages, the non-economic costs and benefits that seem likely to accrue from major alterations in its technological apparatus, and allow these considerations to balance, offset—and on occasion, even to veto—the guide of profitability. Thus the actual impact of science and technology on our social existence will depend not merely on the presence of these overriding forces in our age, but on the influence which we *unavoidably* exert on their social application—including the passive influence of permitting economic criteria to exert their sway largely unchallenged.

The same general conclusion is true with respect to the possibilities of influencing the other main forces which affect our future. There is little doubt, for instance, of the overwhelming power of popular aspirations in the underdeveloped nations, or of the likelihood that those aspirations, in the frustrating conditions of underdevelopment, will lead toward economic collectivism and political dictatorship. But the fact that there is very little we can do about this is very different from saying that we therefore have no control over this aspect of the future. On the contrary, it is only by understanding the "inevitable" outlook that we can hope to devise policies which have some chance of exerting a lasting and positive effect on the course of economic development. Similar alternatives confront us in dealing with the trend of all industrialized nations, ourselves included, toward some form of economic collectivism. To continue to set ourselves adamantly against this trend is to minimize rather than maximize our possible historic influence. The possibility poised by history is not that of denying the advent of planning, but of seizing control of it to assure the kind of collective economic responsibility we want.

Thus the outlook on the future as history does not pave the way for an attitude of passivity and still less for defeatism. Those who would reject the idea of the "inevitable" future for these reasons are in fact more likely to object to the bold measures to which it points as the only means of rescuing our future from the category of "inevitable fate." It is unquestionably true that the exercise of such historic control is fraught with risk. *But so is the exercise of non-control.* The issue is not the simple and clear-cut one of a greater or lesser freedom. It

is the difficult and clouded choice of a subservience to the necessities imposed by the forces visibly at work in our midst, or
the perilous freedom of an exercise of historic control over
ourselves.

How we shall behave in the face of this difficult choice of
historic paths, it is not easy to say. Whether in the end we shall
remain passive before the enveloping changes of history, or
attempt to adapt our institutions so as to minimize their impact,
is a question whose answer inevitably involves subjective
biases. The degree to which the "common sense," the "basic
instincts" of the people can be relied upon, the flexibility and
farsightedness of the powers that be—these are matters about
which purely objective judgments are impossible. All that one
can say is that the challenges are very subtle; that the requisite
changes in institutions, while not revolutionary, are nonetheless very great; and that the required degree of farsightedness
is correspondingly high. Thus it is not difficult to conclude
that the possibilities of historic intervention will not, in fact,
be put to use. A critic who assesses the American scene in terms
of its alertness to the underlying challenges of our times can
scarcely fail to be struck by the general poverty of the prevailing outlook: the men of wealth and power, mentally locked
within their corporate privileges; the middle classes, more
Bourbon than the Bourbons; the working classes, unable to
formulate any social program or purpose beyond "getting
theirs"; the academicians, blind to the irrationalities of the society they seek to rationalize.

Yet it is one of the disconcerting facts of an open society
that it offers so many opportunities for facile generalizations
and so little sure ground for generally valid ones. As long as

there is still visible in American society a continuing evidence of new thought and dissent, a self-control with respect to the use of political power, and above all, a nagging awareness that all is not right, it would be arrogant and unjust to shrug away our future as a hopeless cause. There are, after all, great traditions of responsibility and social flexibility in America. In them there may yet reside the impetus to seize the historic possibilities before us, and to make those changes which may be necessary if the forces of history are not to sweep over us in an uncontrolled and destructive fashion. But it is useless to hope that this will happen so long as we persist in believing that in the future toward which we are blindly careering everything is "possible," or that we can escape the ultimate responsibility of defining our limits of possibility for ourselves.

5. The Idea of Progress

In our last section we have been concerned with the problems of historic possibility and impossibility, of freedom and necessity, which a philosophy of optimism tends to obscure. Now we must turn to a second shortcoming of our traditional outlook on history. This is the tendency of our philosophy to present the workings of the forces of history in an overly simplified manner—a manner which has entirely failed to prepare us for the actual turnings which history has taken. If we are to sum up the shortcoming in a phrase it would be this: *The optimistic philosophy equates the movement of history's forces with the idea of progress.*

Whether there is such a thing as "progress" in history depends, of course, on what we mean by the word. It is clear enough that there has been, particularly in the last three centuries, a steady and cumulative accretion of technical virtuosity and scientific knowledge which permits us to speak of "progress" in these fields in a fairly specific sense. One particularly important aspect of this progress has been the measurable lengthening of the longevity of man and the improvement of his capacity to alleviate his bodily ills. A second instance of definable progress has been in the rise of the level of well-being of the masses in the West—although this can be said to be more than offset by an actual decline, over the last century, of the "well-being" of the teeming masses of the East. A third instance, less easily indexed, but no less demonstrable in the large, is the historic progress from a society in which man is born into his status toward a society in which he is able to define his status for himself.

It is with these aspects of the forces of history that optimism identifies progress, and so long as the meaning of "progress" is restricted to such reasonably definable movements, there can be no objection to the word. But it is also apparent that we cannot generalize from these specific concepts of progress to the larger idea of an all-embracing progress of "society." There is no reason to believe that today's private morality, level of social ethics, and general nobility of public ideals are in any sense superior to much of the recorded past, if indeed they are equal to the best of American Revolutionary times or to the heights reached in the golden ages of Greece and Rome. Our cultural and aesthetic public existence is hardly at an historic high point. And if, with all his gains in health, well-being, or status, the average person is "happier," more serenely or creatively engaged in life than in the past, this is not apparent in the happiness, serenity, or creativity of our age. We often imagine that "life" is much better today than, say, in the Dark Ages, but this depends very much on whose lives we conjure up in these two periods. After all, we live at a time when German brutality reached what may be, statistically, a record for the systematic extermination of life, and when Russian despotism at its worst took us back to the level of morality of the crueler Biblical kings.

Yet these somber considerations do not dispose of the idea of progress. Rather they raise the question: Why is it that the forces of history, which are indisputably the carriers of potentially beneficial political and economic and technological change, have not resulted in a corresponding improvement in the human condition? What are the attributes of these forces, as agents of change, which the optimistic philosophy glosses over? Let us try to identify some of these attributes which are omitted in the optimistic notion of progress.

6. The Inertia of History

Because we live in a time of great change, and because our philosophy of optimism makes us expectant of and receptive to change, we may easily overlook a deeply important aspect of historic development. This is its quality of inertia. It is a quality which is manifest not only in resistance to change—although that is one of its more important aspects—but in the viscosity which is imparted to history because people tend to repeat and continue their ways of life as long as it is possible for them to do so.

We do not usually call inertia to mind when we seek the great molding forces of history. And yet this humble characteristic is responsible for more of "history" than all the campaigns, the movements, the revolutions we readily call to mind. The simple, but quintessential fact that human beings persist in living their lives in familiar ways, which are the only ways they know how, is the very lifeline of social continuity itself.

This inertia which exerts so powerful a drag on history undoubtedly has its biological and psychological roots. But it is more than just an "innate" human characteristic. It is also the outcome of the historic social condition of man. For

193

the persistence of habit acts as a protective reflex for the overwhelming majority of men who know very little except that life is a fragile possession, and that tried and true ways, however onerous, have at least proved capable of sustaining it. A mulish perseverance in old ways is not without reason when life is lived at the brink of existence where a small error may spell disaster. An instance in point was provided some years ago when a team of United Nations agricultural experts sought in vain to persuade Turkish farmers to improve their crops by removing the stones from their fields. Finally a few of the younger ones consented—whereupon, to the chagrin of the experts, their yields promptly *declined*. In the arid climate of Turkey, the stones had served the function of helping to retain the scanty moisture in the soil.[3]

Inertia shows itself as well in a general reluctance to embrace new social ideas. Reformers throughout history have deplored the tenacity with which the privileged classes have clung to their prerogatives—even when it was no longer in their "best interests" to do so. This is not so surprising when we view the enormous gulf which has normally separated the privileged and the unprivileged. What is far more striking is the difficulty which reformers have had in making even the most miserable and oppressed classes "see" the inequity of their lot, and in persuading them to rise in protest. The fact that our historic glance is easily caught by a few *jacqueries* obscures the fact that revolutions are remarkable in history not for their frequency but for their rarity, even though the "normal" condition of man has always been harsh enough to war-

[3] *Cultural Patterns and Technical Change,* ed. Margaret Mead (New York, 1955), p. 186.

rant revolutionary sentiments. We must conclude that whenever it has been possible the human being has *wished* to believe in the rightness and fixity of the situation in which he has found himself.

The inertia of ideologies as well as of institutions is often taken as a lamentable fact. It is the despair of the social engineer, the *bête noir* of the utopian planner. Nonetheless we must remember that there is a constructive role which this inertia also plays. A society without ideological inertia would live from instant to instant in peril of a fatal turning. The fixity of our voting habits, our customary beliefs, our stubbornly held ideas, even when these are wrong, serves a purpose in protecting and stabilizing the community. The reformer who despairs because people will not listen to reason forgets that it is this same suspicion of change which helps to prevent people from heeding the Pied Pipers for whom society never lacks. We may make progress only by freeing ourselves from the rut of the past, but without this rut an orderly society would hardly be possible in the first place.

This historic undertow of inertia warns us against facile conceptions of "progress" in two respects. In the first place it disabuses us of the notion of the "ease" of social change. For most of the world's peoples, who have known only the changelessness of history, such a stress on the difficulty of change would not be necessary. But for ourselves, whose outlook is conditioned by the extraordinary dynamism of our unique historic experience, it is a needed caution. Contrary to our generally accepted belief, change is not the rule but the exception in life. Whether it is imposed from above or imposes itself from below, change must reckon with the reluctance of humankind to relinquish habits not only of a lifetime, but of life itself. This is the reason why even such enormous transformations as those we have dealt with in this book are slow, stretched out over generations, invisible from one day to the next.

Second, the drag of inertia warns us against the overestimation of the effects of change. The optimistic conception of progress calls our attention to the sweeping improvements which can be brought about by technology or democracy or economic advance. All that is certainly true as far as it goes. No one can doubt the capacity of history's forces to legislate beneficial changes in society. But there is a level of social existence to which these forces penetrate last and least. This is the level at which "society" is visible only as the personal and private encounters of each of us with his fellow man. It is the level at which life is *lived*, rather than the level at which it is abstractly conceived.

Here, at this final level of personal experience, the inertia of history is most apparently manifest. It is here that the revolutionary, having brought about tremendous changes in "society," comes to grips with the petty irritations of inefficient colleagues and apathetic clerks, of the "human factor" which like sand in a machine, has wrecked so many well-planned enterprises. It is not that revolutions, or the more gradual changes of historic evolution, make these daily frictions of life any worse. It is rather that so much of life remains the same, regardless of the new boundaries in which it is contained.

In this grinding persistence of the "human factor" lies the reason for much of the disillusion which so frequently follows a passionate attempt to bring about social progress. As Ignazio Silone has written: "Political regimes come and go; bad habits remain."[4] The underlying sameness of life, the reassertion of old established ways, of "bad habits," is an aspect of history which must not be lost to sight amid the more dramatic changes of the superstructure of society. An appreciation of the fact of human inertia must not lead us to understate the extent to which change is possible in society, but it should caution us against identifying this change with the equivalent "progress" of human life at a fundamental level.

7. The Heritage of the Human Condition

We have seen that optimism misleads us with respect to the possibilities of "progress" because it tends to underestimate the difficulty and to overestimate the consequences of historic change. But it compounds that shortcoming with a second and perhaps even more important failure. This is its lack of realism as to our starting point in the making of history. It is its failure to confront truthfully and unflinchingly the condition of the human being as it now exists.

Optimism tacitly views that condition in a favorable light.

[4] "The Choice of Comrades," *Voices of Dissent* (New York, 1958), p. 325.

The very assumption that the growth of technical skill, political equality, or economic well-being will automatically lead to "progress"—rather than to increased destructiveness, heightened social disorder, or vulgar opulence—already takes for granted an environment in which rationality, self-control, and dignity are paramount social attributes.

But this is hardly the impression one gets from an examination of the panorama of human existence. If there is such a thing as an average human being, he is to be found among the majority of mankind which lives in the continents of the East and South. The chasm which divides the average life on these continents from our own is so wide that we can barely imagine existence on the other side. To be an Indian villager, a Chinese peasant, an African mine-worker is to be in a human condition whose dark and narrow confines cannot be penetrated by a Western mind.

But life on our side of the chasm is also very far from presenting a heartening vista. In the United States, for example, preventable disease and even deformity are still widespread. Mental aberration identifiably touches a tenth of the population. Criminality, in various social forms from murder to tax evasion, is prevalent among all classes. The urban environment in which life is mainly lived is crowded, often unspeakably ugly, and in its spreading slums, vicious. The average education is barely adequate to allow the population to cope with the technological complexities of the age, and insufficient to allow all but a few to understand them. Large numbers of families do not know or care how to raise their children, as witness the epidemic incidence of juvenile disorders.

The list could be extended without difficulty. But what characterizes many, if not all of these degradations of life, is that they are unnecessary. Most of them could be vastly alleviated by a sustained and wholehearted effort. Yet such an effort—as to whose immense "value" all would agree—seems impossible to undertake. Indeed, the very suggestion that these areas of need should carry an absolutely overriding priority, taking precedence over any and all more "profitable" activities, smacks of a suspicious radicalism. We are simply not concerned, beyond a mild lip-service, with mounting an all-out effort to raise the level of national health or civic virtue, or mass living conditions or average education or upbringing. Looking at some of the institutions we nourish and defend, it would not be difficult to maintain that our society is an immense stamping press for the careless production of underdeveloped and malformed human beings, and that, whatever it may claim to be, it is not a society fundamentally concerned with moral issues, with serious purposes, or with human dignity.

The point, however, is not to berate ourselves for our obvious failure to produce anything like a "good society." The point is rather that, with all its glaring and inexcusable failures, the United States is still probably the most favored and favorable place on earth for a child to be born and to grow up.

These melancholy facts must assume their rightful place in any evaluation of the prospects for "social progress." For in such a social atmosphere the forces of history do not lead automatically in the direction which optimism assumes. In an atmosphere of neglect of and indifference to human capabilities, it is not at all surprising that technology should result in the trivialization of life and the stultification of work. It is certainly not remarkable that, in the harsh and primitive setting of underdevelopment, popular political aspirations press toward extreme and violent "solutions" to the problems of underdevelopment; nor that, in the more advanced societies, they mold society in the image of the mediocrity of mind and sentiment they represent. Nor, given the prevalence of physical poverty in the backward nations and of psychological poverty in all nations, is the pre-eminence of materialistic drives and goals to be wondered at. In sum, today as in the past, the half-educated, half-emancipated state of human society assures that there will be a long continuation of the violence, the instability, the blatant injustice, which are the most grievous aspects of the human tragedy. This is the true heritage of the human condition, and its bitter legacy.

What is perhaps the most sorrowful aspect of this tragedy is that its victims are chosen arbitrarily and at random. There is no guilt or innocence, no measure of culpability or responsibility in the fate meted out by a world which is still more brute than man. Those who fall in wars do not "start" the wars. The victims of Hitler or Stalin were not those who raised these dictators to power. Nor will there be a fine balancing of accounts when the crimes of South Africa eventually exact their terrible retribution, or when the indignities of the American South work their full damage to the American social fabric. In a world in which conscious morality can be regarded with derision, and reason with suspicion, this random toll of social tragedy cannot be avoided. It is the consequence of a situation in which, as Albert Camus writes in *The*

Fall: "We cannot assert the innocence of anyone, whereas we can state with certainty the guilt of all."

To raise these dark thoughts is not to sermonize that man is "wicked" or to avoid the conclusion that some men are much more guilty than others. Neither is it to maintain that there is no hope for a betterment of the human condition. On the contrary, there is today a greater long-term prospect for such betterment than humanity has ever known before. But the heritage of the past is too deep to be overcome in a matter of a few generations. It will be a long while until the human condition has been substantially improved. Not to face up to this fact with compassion and concern is only to cringe before reality. And while this should urge us on with all the strength at our command to support every effort to improve the condition of man, it cannot but chasten us as to the reasonable expectations of the "progress" which that condition will permit.

8. *The Ambiguity of Events*

In the very idea of progress, as we commonly accept it, is contained the notion of goals. We strive for specific objectives, located in the future, and imagine that each objective gained is a recognizable step toward "progress." As a result we find ourselves confounded when, having reached an objective, what we encounter is not the "progress" we anticipated but a new set of problems stemming from the very advance itself.

This disconcerting aspect of experience can be described as the ambiguity of events. By this we mean that every event in history has a Januslike quality—one face which regards the past, and one which looks ahead; one aspect which is the culmination of what has gone before, and another which is the point of departure for what is to follow.

Simplistic ideas of progress see only the near face of events when they look to the future. Hence such views of the future typically underrate its complexities. They do not consider that the solution of one problem is only the formulation of the next. What an awareness of the ambiguity of events thus subtracts from the optimistic view of progress is the luxury of believing that progress is a simple pyramiding of success. The two-sided nature of future events does not deny that our problems may be our opportunities but it asserts with equal conviction that our opportunities may become our problems.

There is no more dramatic example of this than the impact on world history of that most "unambiguous" of all evidences of progress: the development of modern medicine. It is not necessary to spell out the enormous benefits which medical science has brought to mankind. Yet no assessment of the over-all impact of modern medicine on our age can ignore the fact that it has also been the "cause" of an immense amount of additional suffering in the world. By its success in reducing the scourges of mass disease and infant mortality, the "progress" of medical science has crowded the already overpopulated villages and cities of Asia and South America with still more mouths, and has thus aggravated the very human suffering it set out to relieve.

Needless to say, not every instance of progress cancels itself out in so direct and distressing a fashion as this. The point, rather, is that progress does not merely consist in the surmounting of a previous problem, but inherently consists in the emergence of a new problem which, although different, may be quite as grave as the old. In the course of this book, for example, we have seen such new problems emerging from the advance of technology or from the achievement of abundance in our own society. These new problems do not gainsay the advances which technology or economic growth bring us. But it may well be that the consequences of our technological captivity, or the control problems of economic abundance will be just as humanly crushing as the problems of insufficiency or technical inadequacy from whose solution they emerged. There is no reason to believe that the successive problems of "progress" pose easier challenges; indeed it is probable that the overcoming of the "simpler" problems of poverty and disease opens the doors on progressively more profound, elusive, and insoluble human dilemmas.

Marx and Hegel called this ambiguous aspect of progress the dialectic of history. Marx, however, brought his dialectical analysis to a halt with the achievement of communism as the "terminus" of the history of class struggle. Ironically enough, it is probable that there is no aspect of future history which today more desperately needs dialectical clarification than the achievement of the communist—or for the West, the socialist—goal. It is clear that as the "near side" of socialism approaches, it is the "far side" which becomes of ever greater interest and importance. To consider socialism as a "goal" of social history is to fall prey to the optimistic delusion that goals are milestones in history from which the next stage of development promises to be "easier" or unambiguously "better" than the past. To rid oneself of this comforting notion is not to lessen one's ardor to resolve the difficulties of the present, but to arm oneself realistically for the continuance of the human struggle in the future.

9. The Grand Dynamic of History

Is there then no possibility for progress?

As it must by now be clear, much depends on what one means by the question. If by "progress" we mean a fundamental elevation in the human estate, a noticeable movement of society in the direction of the ideals of Western humanism, a qualitative as well as a quantitative betterment of the condition of man, it is plain that we must put away our ideas of progress over the foreseeable vista of the historic future. For whereas there is no question but that the forces of our time are bringing about momentous and profound changes, it is only optimistic self-deception to anticipate, or even to wish for, the near advent of a perceptibly "better" world as a result. Taking into account the human condition as it now exists, the laggard slowness with which improvements in institutions are followed by improvements in "life," the blurred and ambiguous fashion in which history passes from problem to problem, it is certain enough that the tenor of world history will remain much as it is for a long while to come.

Indeed, from the point of view of the West and especially of America, it may seem to be deteriorating. As we have seen through the pages of this book, many of the tendencies of world history are likely to manifest themselves to us as a worsening of the outlook. We may well be tempted to interpret this growing intractability of the environment as the metamorphosis of progress into retrogression.

Against this dark horizon it is hardly possible to cling to the sanguine hopes and complacent expectations of the past. And yet if we can lift our gaze beyond the confines of our own situation, it is possible to see that every one of these changes is essential and inescapable if the present condition of humankind is to be surpassed. Until the avoidable evils of society have been redressed, or at least made the target of the wholehearted effort of the organized human community, it is not only premature but presumptuous to talk of "the dignity of the individual." The ugly, obvious, and terrible wounds of mankind must be dressed and allowed to heal before we can begin to know the capacities, much less enlarge the vision, of the human race as a whole.

In the present state of world history the transformations which are everywhere at work are performing this massive and crude surgery. We have dwelt sufficiently in the preceding pages on the violence and cruelty, the humanly deforming aspects of the changes about us. Now we must see that in their

205

ultimate impact on history it is the positive side of these great transformations which must be stressed. However unruly the revolution of the underdeveloped nations, it is nonetheless the commencement of a movement away from the squalor and apathy which three-quarters of the human race still consider to be life. With all its disregard for Western standards of justice and liberty, the forced march of communism is nevertheless retreading the essential, but now forgotten path of early industrial development of the West. Whatever its capacity for the destruction or the diminution of man, the perfection and application of industrial technology is withal the only possible escape from the historic indenture of man. And no matter what its difficulties, the painful evolution beyond present-day capitalism is indispensable if those nations which have gained the benefits of material wealth are now to cope rationally with its administration.

Thus the blind and often brutal impact of the historic forces of our day can still be said to point in the direction of optimism and of progress. Only in our present situation, the West is no longer the spearhead of those forces, but their target. What is at bottom a movement of hope and well-being for the inarticulate and inadequate masses of mankind is a fearful threat to the delicate and now gravely exposed civilization of the articulate and advanced few.

No member of the Western community who loves its great achievements and who has enjoyed the inestimable value of its liberties and values can confront this outlook of history without anguish. Of all those who will feel the blows of the future, none will suffer more than the heirs of the long tradition of Western humanism, and none will more acutely feel the delays and the recession of "progress" as the world endures its protracted ordeal.

More aware than the rising masses of the world of the destination to which their inchoate revolution may hopefully carry them, it is the humanist spirits of the West who will feel most betrayed by the violence and excess which will likely accompany its course. Ever hopeful of the re-entry of the communist nations into the Western community of thought, it is the Western intellectuals and idealists who will bear the full agony of watching for and waiting for signs of change which may be very long in coming. Alive to the immense potential benefits of the technical virtuosity of their age, it is again the guardians of the humanist tradition who will most despair at its continued misapplication; just as it will be they rather than the masses who will wish for a more responsible form of economic society and who will chafe at the continuance of the old order.

This prospect of disappointment and delay may give rise to a tragedy greater than the tragic events of history itself. This would be the disillusion of Western thought and the abandonment of its hopes for and its distant vision of progress. It would be the surrender of the very ideals of the West before the crushing advent of history, and the adoption of an indifference, or worse, a cynicism before the march of events.

If this tragedy is to be avoided, the West will have need of two qualities: fortitude and understanding. It must come to see that because this is not a time of fulfillment does not mean that it is a time of waste. It is rather a time when the West must take upon itself a new and more difficult role in history than in the past: not that of leading in the van of history's forces under the banner of progress, but that of preserving from the ruthless onslaught of history's forces the integrity of the very idea of progress itself.

Particularly for Americans will this long period of abeyance provide a test of the spirit. Accustomed by our historic training to expect a mastery over events which is no longer possible, we are apt to interpret the intransigence of history as a kind of personal betrayal rather than as a vast and impersonal process of worldwide evolution. Thus there is the danger that we may abandon our optimism for a black and bitter pessimism, or for a kind of "heroic" defiance.

But neither pessimism nor defiance, any more than optimism, will give us the fortitude and understanding we require. For this we need an attitude which accepts the outlook of the historic future without succumbing to false hopes or to an equally false despair; a point of view which sees in the juggernaut of history's forces both the means by which progress painfully made in the past may be trampled underfoot, and the means by which a broader and stronger base for progress in the future may be brought into being.

Such an attitude may retain its kernel of optimism. But more is needed for the display of stoic fortitude than a residual faith in the idea of progress. Above all there is required an understanding of the grand dynamic of history's forces in preparing the way for eventual progress. There is needed a broad and compassionate comprehension of the history-shaking transformations now in mid-career, of their combined work of demolition and construction, of the hope they embody and the price they will exact. Only from such a sense of historic understanding can come the strength to pass through the gauntlet with an integrity of mind and spirit.

What is tragically characteristic of our lives today is an absence of just such an understanding. It is very difficult while America and the West are at bay to feel a sense of positive identification with the forces that are preparing the environment of the future. Less and less are we able to locate our lives meaningfully in the pageant of history. More and more do we find ourselves retreating to the sanctuary of an insulated individualism, sealed off in our private concerns from the larger events which surround us.

Such an historic disorientation and disengagement is a terrible private as well as public deprivation. In an age which no longer waits patiently through this life for the rewards of the next, it is a crushing spiritual blow to lose one's sense of participation in mankind's journey, and to see only a huge milling-around, a collective living-out of lives with no larger purpose than the days which each accumulates. When we estrange ourselves from history we do not enlarge, we diminish ourselves, even as individuals. We subtract from our lives one meaning which they do in fact possess, whether we recognize it or not. We cannot help living in history. We can only fail to be aware of it. If we are to meet, endure, and transcend the trials and defeats of the future—for trials and defeats there are certain to be—it can only be from a point of view which, seeing the future as part of the sweep of history, enables us to establish our place in that immense procession in which is incorporated whatever hope humankind may have.

ACKNOWLEDGMENTS

It is pleasant to acknowledge my gratitude once again to Dr. Adolph Lowe of the Graduate Faculty of the New School for Social Research. There is not a page of this book which has not benefited from his criticism; and beyond that, without his moral as well as intellectual encouragement the entire project might have been given up many times. I am proud to express my indebtedness to him.

Many other friends have read the manuscript at various stages and have given me the benefit of their counsel. Needless to say they are not responsible for the arguments and ideas of the book, but their suggestions have contributed immeasurably to my final formulations and have prevented me from making many egregious errors. In particular I should like to thank Moses Abramovitz, Henry Aubrey, Peter Bernstein, Morton Hunt, Joseph Kraft, and Paul Sweezy. And Miss Violet Serwin is due a special note of thanks for an immaculate manuscript prepared from a nearly illegible draft.

Finally I must express my gratitude to my wife, not only for a painstaking critique of style and lucidity, but even more for a loving good nature and forbearance without which the task would have been doubly hard; and to record for posterity that without Peter and David, for whom this book was written, the task would have been much easier, but much less pleasant.

Robert L. Heilbroner

Chilmark, Mass.
August 20, 1959

211

INDEX

213

hARPER ⚡ τORChBOOKS

† The New American Nation Series, edited by Henry Steele Commager and Richard B. Morris.
‡ American Perspectives series, edited by Bernard Wishy and William E. Leuchtenburg.
α History of Europe series, edited by J. H. Plumb.
§ The Library of Religion and Culture, edited by Benjamin Nelson.
‖ Researches in the Social, Cultural, and Behavioral Sciences, edited by Benjamin Nelson.
Σ Harper Modern Science Series, edited by James A. Newman.
° Not for sale in Canada.
+ Documentary History of the United States series, edited by Richard B. Morris.
# Documentary History of Western Civilization series, edited by Eugene C. Black and Leonard W. Levy.
Λ The Economic History of the United States series, edited by Henry David et al.
¶ European Perspectives series, edited by Eugene C. Black.
** Contemporary Essays series, edited by Leonard W. Levy.
* The Stratum Series, edited by John Hale.

2

3

R. H. TAWNEY: The Agrarian Problem in the Sixteenth Century. *Intro. by Lawrence Stone* TB/1315

H. R. TREVOR-ROPER: The European Witch-craze of the Sixteenth and Seventeenth Centuries and Other Essays ° TB/1416

VESPASIANO: Rennaissance Princes, Popes, and XVth Century: *The Vespasiano Memoirs. Introduction by Myron P. Gilmore. Illus.* TB/1111

History: Modern European

RENE ALBRECHT-CARRIE, Ed.: The Concert of Europe # HR/1341

MAX BELOFF: The Age of Absolutism, 1660-1815 TB/1062

OTTO VON BISMARCK: Reflections and Reminiscences. *Ed. with Intro. by Theodore S. Hamerow* ¶ TB/1357

EUGENE C. BLACK, Ed.: British Politics in the Nineteenth Century # HR/1427

D. W. BROGAN: The Development of Modern France ° Vol. 1: *From the Fall of the Empire to the Dreyfus Affair* TB/1184
Vol. II: *The Shadow of War, World War I, Between the Two Wars* TB/1185

ALAN BULLOCK: Hitler, A Study in Tyranny. ° *Revised Edition. Iuus.* TB/1123

GORDON A. CRAIG: From Bismarck to Adenauer: *Aspects of German Statecraft. Revised Edition* TB/1171

LESTER G. CROCKER, Ed.: The Age of Enlightenment # HR/1423

JACQUES DROZ: Europe between Revolutions, 1815-1848. ° *a Trans. by Robert Baldick* TB/1346

JOHANN GOTTLIEB FICHTE: Addresses to the German Nation. *Ed. with Intro. by George A. Kelly* ¶ TB/1366

ROBERT & ELBORG FORSTER, Eds.: European Society in the Eighteenth Century # HR/1404

C. C. GILLISPIE: Genesis and Geology: *The Decades before Darwin* § TB/51

ALBERT GOODWIN: The French Revolution TB/1064

JOHN B. HALSTED, Ed.: Romanticism # HR/1387

STANLEY HOFFMANN et al.: In Search of France: *The Economy, Society and Political System In the Twentieth Century* TB/1219

H. STUART HUGHES: The Obstructed Path: *French Social Thought in the Years of Desperation* TB/1451

JOHAN HUIZINGA: Dutch Civilisation in the 17th Century and Other Essays ° TB/1453

WALTER LAQUEUR & GEORGE L. MOSSE, Eds.: Education and Social Structure in the 20th Century. ° *Volume 6 of the* Journal of Contemporary History TB/1339

WALTER LAQUEUR & GEORGE L. MOSSE, Ed.: International Fascism, 1920 1945. ° *Volume 1 of the* Journal of Contemporary History TB/1276

WALTER LAQUEUR & GEORGE L. MOSSE, Eds.: Literature and Politics in the 20th Century. ° *Volume 5 of the* Journal of Contemporary History. TB/1328

WALTER LAQUEUR & GEORGE L. MOSSE, Eds.: The New History: *Trends in Historical Research and Writing Since World War II. ° Volume 4 of the* Journal of Contemporary History TB/1327

WALTER LAQUEUR & GEORGE L. MOSSE, Eds.: 1914: *The Coming of the First World War. ° Volume3 of the* Journal of Contemporary History TB/1306

JOHN MCMANNERS: European History, 1789-1914: *Men, Machines and Freedom* TB/1419

PAUL MANTOUX: The Industrial Revolution in the Eighteenth Century: *An Outline of the Beginnings of the Modern Factory System in England* TB/1079

KINGSLEY MARTIN: French Liberal Thought in the Eighteenth Century: *A Study of Political Ideas from Bayle to Condorcet* TB/1114

NAPOLEON III: Napoleonic Ideas: *Des Idées Napoléoniennes, par le Prince Napoléon-Louis Bonaparte. Ed. by Brison D. Gooch* ¶ TB/1336

FRANZ NEUMANN: Behemoth: *The Structure and Practice of National Socialism, 1933-1944* TB/1289

DAVID OGG: Europe of the Ancien Régime, 1783 ° *a* TB/1271

GEORGE RUDE: Revolutionary Europe, 1783-1815 ° *a* TB/1272

MASSIMO SALVADORI, Ed.: Modern Socialism # TB/1374

DENIS MACK SMITH, Ed.: The Making of Italy, 1796-1870 # HR/1356

ALBERT SOREL: Europe Under the Old Regime, *Translated by Francis H. Herrick* TB/1121

ROLAND N. STROMBERG, Ed.: Realsim, Naturalism, and Symbolism: *Modes of Thought and Expression in Europe, 1848-1914* # IIR/1355

A. J. P. TAYLOR: From Napoleon to Lenin: *Historical Essays* ° TB/1268

A. J. P. TAYLOR: The Habsburg Monarchy, 1809-1918: *A History of the Austrian Empire and Austria-Hungary* ° TB/1187

J. M. THOMPSON: European History, 1494-1789 TB/1431

DAVID THOMSON, Ed.: France: Empire and Republic, 1850-1940 # HR/1387

H. R. TREVOR-ROPER: Historical Essays TR/1269

W. WARREN WAGAR, Ed.: Science, Faith, and MAN: *European Thought Since 1914* # HR/1362

MACK WALKER, Ed.: Metternich's Europe, 1813-1848 # HR/1361

ELIZABETH WISKEMANN: Europe of the Dictators, 1919-1945 ° *a* TB/1273

JOHN B. WOLF: France: 1814-1919: *The Rise of a Liberal-Democratic Society* TB/3019

Literature & Literary Criticism

JACQUES BARZUN: The House of Intellect TB/1051

W. J. BATE: From Classic to Romantic: *Premises of Taste in Eighteenth Century England* TB/1036

VAN WYCK BROOKS: Van Wyck Brooks: The Early Years: *A Selection from his Works, 1908-1921 Ed. with Intro. by Claire Sprague* TB/3082

RICHMOND LATTIMORE, Translator: The Odyssey of Homer TB/1389

ROBERT PREYER, Ed.: Victorian Literature ** TR/1302

BASIL WILEY: Nineteenth Century Studies: *Coleridge to Matthew Arnold* ° TB/1261

RAYMOND WILLIAMS: Culture and Society, 1780-1950 ° TB/1252

Philosophy

HENRI BERGSON: Time and Free Will: *An Essay on the Immediate Data of Consciousness* ° TB/1021

LUDWIG BINSWANGER: Being-in-the-World: *Selected Papers. Trans. with Intro. by Jacob Needleman* TB/1365

H. J. BLACKHAM: Six Existentialist Thinkers: *Kierkegaard, Nietzsche, Jaspers, Marcel, Heidegger, Sartre* ° TB/1002

6

MARTIN BUBER: Eclipse of God: *Studies in the Relation Between Religion and Philosophy* TB/12

MARTIN BUBER: Hasidism and Modern Man. *Edited and Translated by Maurice Friedman* TB/839

MARTIN BUBER: The Knowledge of Man. *Edited with an Introduction by Maurice Friedman. Translated by Maurice Friedman and Ronald Gregor Smith* TB/135

MARTIN BUBER: Moses. *The Revelation and the Covenant* TB/837

MARTIN BUBER: The Origin and Meaning of Hasidism. *Edited and Translated by Maurice Friedman* TB/835

MARTIN BUBER: The Prophetic Faith TB/73

MARTIN BUBER: Two Types of Faith: *Interpenetration of Judaism and Christianity* ° TB/75

MALCOLM L. DIAMOND: Martin Buber: *Jewish Existentialist* TB/840

M. S. ENSLIN: Christian Beginnings TB/5

M. S. ENSLIN: The Literature of the Christian Movement TB/6

HENRI FRANKFORT: Ancient Egyptian Religion: *An Interpretation* TB/77

MAURICE S. FRIEDMAN: Martin Buber: *The Life of Dialogue* TB/64

ABRAHAM HESCHEL: The Earth Is the Lord's & The Sabbath. *Two Essays* TB/828

ABRAHAM HESCHEL: God in Search of Man: *A Philosophy of Judaism* TB/807

ABRAHAM HESCHEL: Man Is not Alone: *A Philosophy of Religion* TB/838

ABRAHAM HESCHEL: The Prophets: *An Introduction* TB/1421

T. J. MEEK: Hebrew Origins TB/69

JAMES MUILENBURG: The Way of Israel: *Biblical Faith and Ethics* TB/133

H. H. ROWLEY: The Growth of the Old Testament TB/107

D. WINTON THOMAS, Ed.: Documents from Old Testament Times TB/85

Religion: Early Christianity Through Reformation

ANSELM OF CANTERBURY: Truth, Freedom, and Evil: *Three Philosophical Dialogues. Edited and Translated by Jasper Hopkins and Herbert Richardson* TB/317

MARSHALL W. BALDWIN, Ed.: Christianity through the 13th Century # HR/1468

ADOLF DEISSMAN: Paul: *A Study in Social and Religious History* TB/15

EDGAR J. GOODSPEED: A Life of Jesus TB/1

ROBERT M. GRANT: Gnosticism and Early Christianity TB/136

WILLIAM HALLER: The Rise of Puritanism TB/22

ARTHUR DARBY NOCK: St. Paul ° TR/104

GORDON RUPP: Luther's Progress to the Diet of Worms ° TB/120

Religion: The Protestant Tradition

KARL BARTH: Church Dogmatics: *A Selection. Intro. by H. Gollwitzer. Ed. by G. W. Bromiley* TB/95

KARL BARTH: Dogmatics in Outline TB/56

KARL BARTH: The Word of God and the Word of Man TB/13

WHITNEY R. CROSS: The Burned-Over District: *The Social and Intellectual History of Enthusiastic Religion in Western New York, 1800-1850* TB/1242

WILLIAM R. HUTCHISON, Ed.: American Protestant Thought: *The Liberal Era* ‡ TB/1385

SOREN KIERKEGAARD: The Journals of Kierkegaard. ° *Edited with an Intro. by Alexander Dru* TB/52

SOREN KIERKEGAARD: The Point of View for My Work as an Author: *A Report to History.* § *Preface by Benjamin Nelson* TB/88

SOREN KIERKEGAARD: The Present Age. § *Translated and edited by Alexander Dru. Introduction by Walter Kaufmann* TB/94

SOREN KIERKEGAARD: Purity of Heart. *Trans. by Douglas Steere* TB/4

SOREN KIERKEGAARD: Repetition: *An Essay in Experimental Psychology* § TB/117

SOREN KIERKEGAARD: Works of Love: *Some Christian Reflections in the Form of Discourses* TB/122

WOLFHART PANNENBERG, et al.: History and Hermeneutic. *Volume 4 of Journal for Theology and the Church, edited by Robert W. Funk and Gerhard Ebeling* TB/254

F. SCHLEIERMACHER: The Christian Faith. *Introduction by Richard R. Niebuhr.*
Vol. I TB/108; Vol. II TB/109

F. SCHLEIERMACHER: On Religion: *Speeches to Its Cultured Despisers. Intro. by Rudolf Otto* TB/36

PAUL TILLICH: Dynamics of Faith TB/42

PAUL TILLICH: Morality and Beyond TB/142

Religion: The Roman & Eastern Christian Traditions

A. ROBERT CAPONIGRI, Ed.: Modern Catholic Thinkers II: *The Church and the Political Order* TB/307

G. P. FEDOTOV: The Russian Religious Mind: *Kievan Christianity, the tenth to the thirteenth Centuries* TB/370

GABRIEL MARCEL: Being and Having: *An Existential Diary. Introduction by James Collins* TB/310

GABRIEL MARCEL: Homo Viator: *Introduction to a Metaphysic of Hope* TB/397

Religion: Oriental Religions

TOR ANDRAE: Mohammed: *The Man and His Faith* § TB/62

EDWARD CONZE: Buddhism: *Its Essence and Development.* ° *Foreword by Arthur Waley* TB/58

EDWARD CONZE: Buddhist Meditation TB/1442

EDWARD CONZE et al, Editors: Buddhist Texts through the Ages TB/113

ANANDA COOMARASWAMY: Buddha and the Gospel of Buddhism TB/119

H. G. CREEL: Confucius and the Chinese Way TB/63

FRANKLIN EDGERTON, Trans. & Ed.: The Bhagavad Gita TB/115

SWAMI NIKHILANANDA, Trans. & Ed.: The Upanishads TB/114

Religion: Philosophy, Culture, and Society

NICOLAS BERDYAEV: The Destiny of Man TB/61

RUDOLF BULTMANN: History and Eschatology: *The Presence of Eternity* ° TB/91

RUDOLF BULTMANN and FIVE CRITICS: Kerygma and Myth: *A Theological Debate* TB/80

RUDOLF BULTMANN and KARL KUNDSIN: Form search. *Trans. by F. C. Grant* TB/96

LUDWIG FEUERBACH: The Essence of Christianity. § *Introduction by Karl Barth. Foreword by H. Richard Niebuhr* TB/11

KYLE HASELDEN: The Racial Problem in Christian Perspective TB/116